The Last Pearl Diver

By Paul Larkin

To GERRY

FOREVER
AND
EVER

ISBN 978-1-291-28084-5

For all those who suffer every minute
of every day of every year, don't let go.

Until they clear the harbour the boats are propelled by heavy oars, each pulled by two men, who sing the song of the pearlers as they row. Often the fleet returns at night when the moon and the tide are full. The sound of the sailors chanting and the splash of the oars is carried across the still water to the town. The sight of hundreds of white sails, some of them coloured orange by the light of the fires burning on the decks, is one of the most picturesque in the world.

Mechanical apparatus of any kind is forbidden, and the methods of diving have not changed since they were described by fourteenth-century travellers. Each diver wears a clip like a clothes-peg to close his nostrils, leather sheaths protect his fingers and enable him to (wrench) the shells from the rocks underneath the sea, and each of his big toes is guarded by a similar sheath. He descends on a rope which has a stone weight attached to it. This is hauled up when he reaches the bottom. Round his neck is slung a string bag, which he fills with shells, attached to a rope with which his comrade, the puller, draws him up again when he gives the signal. Divers remain below the surface for nearly a minute and a half, and they descend about 30 times in one day, often to a depth of 14 fathoms. The shells are heaped on deck during the day and opened in the evening under the vigilant eye of the captain, who puts away the pearls in his sea chest. No diver knows whether it is his shell that contained a pearl. While the men are working they take neither food nor drink, but they eat in the early morning and after sunset they have a meal of rice and dates and fish. The shells are thrown back into the sea, the divers believing that oysters feed upon the empty shells. They believe too, that drops of rain which are caught by the oysters at night form pearls.

The work is very strenuous and conditions are hard, but the divers on the whole are healthy and many of them show unusually fine muscular development. The men are paid no wages, but they receive a share in the profits of the season. Divers are entitled to twice the amount which is paid to a puller, as their work is more arduous. There are several different diving systems, and all of them are very ancient...

Pearl Diving Records of Dubai 1761 - 1960

"Pearl Diver" Scottish Rhyming Slang for Five Pounds in Sterling.

A note from the Author.

Despite there being several known names and situations, this book is a work of fiction. The passages in relation to the Celtic board in 1994 are based on information sourced from employees of the club at that time. It is not meant, in any way, to upset or misinform. The characters in the Sidney story are totally fictional. Whilst certain people will recognise aspects of all the characters, and the fact some are loosely based on people I know, none of these characters actually exist. At least, not under those names...

Paul Larkin
February 2013

For Kim Petrie, Steph O'Neill and Lynn Murphy

Strong ladies with huge hearts who act as daily reminders of how important they are. Which, as men, we need sometimes.

Also for Pat Keenan, a man amongst men.

1

Oh let the sun beat down upon my face.

In life, there can be few more demoralising things than going up to sign oan with yer auld man. It was my auld man who put me wide as to how the brew works:

"Get in there, speak when spoken tae, never let on tae any cunt and never tell them yer ill"

It's a depressing bus journey up there, I had tae tap the fares and my auld man has already declared that he has nae money til he gets his giro. Bleak man. Thankfully the bus stop isnae far from the hoose, or I'd have hud tae listen to him going on the way tae that tae. I wish the brew hud given us different signing on days but we were both Thursday signers, Saturday giros which did have its benefits if you'll pardon the pun. Gitting yer giro on a Saturday morning gave you a full wad for the fitba that day, although that was a load of shite the now, at least the game is in Edinburgh this Saturday, Hibs at Easter Road. It was a good March for us, four wins against Hearts, Hibs, Rangers and Dundee Utd. Still, we couldnae relax could we, no wi the possibility still lingering of *them* winning the European Cup.

Arriving at High Riggs, there's aboot eight cunts in the queue in front of us, my old man scowls at one of the cunts signing folk on, whispers to me "Watch that cunt, he's a right fucking pig". We wait aboot 10 minutes and I get taken first, pit my book down and the boy says to me "How's your job search going?" Great question that, it's designed to make you not be able to answer yes or no yet it completely overlooks the fact that if your job search was going well, you wouldnae fucking be here. "Aye it's going ok, went round the building sites doon Lothian Road and Morrison Street and was telt to come back in a fortnight" The cunt looks satisfied with this and tells me to do the same here. Oscar Wilde this cunt.

I look round and see my auld man at the door with that look that says "Let's get tae fuck" and so I pass all the rows of jobs on the walls and walk past him, telling him I've got a letter to post. "Letter? tae whae? is it a joab like?" I tell him that I was reading a magazine last week and there was a section for pen pals in it and I saw an address in America and decided to try it. He looked at me like I'd told him I'd decided to become a Transvestite and was doing the afternoon shift at the nearby Tipplers. "Aye, right then" was about as good as it got. I hadn't sealed the envelope yet so when we parted ways on Earl Grey Street I pulled out the letter again and looked at again. Studying it like. This was the first letter I had ever written in my life, certainly as an adult. I wisnae even sure why I was daeing this, escapism probably. The grim reality of Thatcher's Britain had been replaced with the grey and dull coloured Major's Mogadon. I left the school four years ago in May and in that time I've worked the sole total of nine months and three days, no consecutively either.

I look at the letter again, should I just toss the fucking thing? I tapped two quid for my bus fares, even though they are only a pound, so I can afford the stamp but I'm still no sure whether to send it or no. I'm also no sure why I have came up here as I've nae idea where the post office is until I spy one opposite the Illicit Still and walk over. As it's after three o'clock the place is rammed as it's full of cunts cashing giros that were not sent to them like they should have been. That's the down side of the Saturday giro, if it disnae come that morning, yer fucked til the Monday and even then yer no getting one over the counter til 3pm. That time period fae around 1pm on the Saturday afternoon, when you know the postie would huv been by now, until 3pm on the Monday, when you risk your life cashing it at a strange post office, is longer than the five years that cunt Fyodor Dostoyevsky did in that Siberian jail. Honestly. I'm aboot tae step in the post office when I look at the letter again

Dear Ferris,

My name is Sidney Dempsey and I'm 19 years old (20 in July though) My mates call me Sid and I am named after My Ma's favourite singer (who you willnae know) which still rankles with my auld man as he's a big Elvis fan but I'll take Sidney before Elvis (The name no the singer). I live in Edinburgh which is in Scotland. I'm single, unemployed and support Celtic (Soccer team). I'm intae music and films, my favourite band is Madness and my favourite film is Scent of a Woman. I've never been to America but hope to one day.

Take care pal

Sid

PS Do you have fitba (Soccer) teams in Philadelphia?

Fuck it, I buy the stamp, lick it and post it in the big red box. I'm oot the door and the weather has gone really nice. I decide to walk down Lothian Road with the intention of walking all the way home and giving myself over a pound to last me til Saturday morning.

That might even rise to over a fiver as ah realise av no visited my Nana this week and, mood dependent, she sometimes gies me a fiver. So I bypass the hoose and head for hers until I pass the windae and see that either one of her pals or her sister in, and no amount of money is worth the feeling of no being wanted that I'd get as soon she answered the door and saw me. My Nana is funny like that, she can be really kind tae ye, gieing ye money and sweets and aw that but sometimes it's like she disnae even want ye there. Moody as fuck. Then again, she hus put up wi ma Grandfaither all this time. That cannie be easy. I decided to plod on doon Pennywell Road and check if my mate Harry is in. I'm meeting him on Saturday for the game, well gawn doon for him like, then we are heading to Pearce's early doors. He's on the brew as well but has got a wee job labouring for his Uncle the now so is rolling in it. Last week I went to his house on a Friday night and his auld man, Big Harry, let me in and cunt was gaga'd on his bed. He wakes up and is like "Awright man, fancy a Pizza?" I telt him I was skint but to be fair he replied "Plenty hiries here, dinnae worry aboot it like" and he phoned it like. It was aw fine til he fell asleep again and the stair buzzer fucking went and I didnae have a bolt to pay it so I hud tae go through the cunt's pockets for the money praying he didnae wake up and try tae set aboot me for robbing him like. Of course he never woke up and when I went to his hoose the next day, he hudnae even eaten his half of the pizza either like.

I press his buzzer but, as usual, there's nae answer. I batter the stair door and it opens and I go up to his hoose but soon as I get there I can tell he's no in. I leave and am going down the stair when I hear some cunt coming up and it's Harry "Alright gadgie?" The cunt has been at The Gunner, I can tell. I tell him that I jist came roond to check that it was still the same for Saturday, 830 at his hoose for a 9pm start at Pearces in Montgomery Street "Aye, that's barry aye. I'll need to go in and get bath now like" I'm sure the cunt is trying to rub it in that he's working and I'm no but I leave it. See the thing is it's hard tae imagine Harry being up at that time on a Saturday but there's drink and fitba involved so if he's no up for that, he's no up for anything. I bound downstairs and into the mecca of Muirhouse Shopping Centre. Check the watch, 5.45pm, I could go down to my mate Martin's but it's always a gamble as he has a lot of nippy younger brothers. I'm still thinking about this when Harry comes oot his stair and goes "Here, I forgot tae tell ye, mind that Race Night ye asked me tae go tae the morn? I can go" Fuck, I'd forgot aw aboot that. Aye, well, see the thing is I... "Dinnae worry aboot it, I'll sub ye £30 an ye can pay me back whenever like" Aye, that sounds fair. Ya fucking beauty, oot the morn's night. With that in mind, I spring in the step it up Kibbys Hill and feel good enough to go back to the hoose to face the auld lady and my faither. I get in just as the sport is on the STV news and the mere mention of Liam Brady has my auld man's blood pressure rising. In all honesty, he has been in a bad mood for a fortnight since The Grand National was cancelled due to a false start. "That cunt better get his finger oot soon, four years in a row of this pish" But Dad, Liam Brady only took over in 1991? "Aye, fae the real King Billy, a man that should niver be sacked fae Celtic" I watch the rest of the sport and Alex Miller appears on it which will enrage Harry if he's watching it as he hates the cunt. Hibs huvnae beat Hearts in a long, long time so I can see his point. I huv my tea, which is one of they shitey frozen pizzas my Ma ey buys and I protest but she just says to me that if I'm no happy, I should pay mair dig money. The standard Marion Dempsey reply. I melt upstairs and put the radio on, the prick Mark Goodier is on, him that does the charts on a Sunday but I keep listening as John Peel is on at 10. I always fall asleep before slavering Bob Harris comes on at midnight.

Board Meeting, Celtic Park, February 4th 1994.

"I call this board meeting at 3.03pm, well its 3.04pm"

"Kevin, can we get on with it please?

Michael Kelly was not in a patient mood.

"I'll just begin by saying, if that's ok with you Kevin?"

Kevin looked irked but nodded.

"Right, we have the obvious disappointment of going out the cup at Motherwell on Saturday, which kills potential lucrative income streams"

"Obvious disappointment? It was a fucking disaster"

"Ok Tom, but we have to move forward. Now David and I are working on something big, can't say too much but you'll know about it soon"

"A player? We need a striker, is Patrick McAvennie available?"

"We let him go last year Jimmy. Now just stick with us for now, this will be huge for Celtic"

Silence went across the room, before Jack McGinn said:

"It will need to be"

2

The next morning I woke up about 20 past 8 and Simon
Mayo was on the Radio 1. Tadger. I lay in my bed til my Ma
left the hoose then went doonstairs where my old man
wasn't in but my hopes were dashed of him being oot aw
day when I noticed the dug was away as well and that
means he's still skint, he's nae work on the day and he
won't be oot too long. I eat a quick bowl of Coco Pops,
waiting a wee bit til the milk goes broon then I go up and
get dressed. I don't chance having a bath even though I
want one because if the cunt comes in when I'm in it, that's
mair grief. Bleak man. Efter getting dressed I pick up my
fags and head out, it's another decent day and so I decide to
head along to my Nana's for a second bite at that fiver. As I
approach the hoose I see my Grandad in the gairden. The
cunt is deef as a post so I'm standing there a couple of
minutes before he clocks me as he wipes his nose. "I was
jist pilling thae weeds there, they get earlier ivry year"
Right. I spy my Nana at the windae, over-seeing his work
like a Foreman but she waves at me to come in so I dae. I sit
doon on their couch and see the time 10.23, so there's no
chance of the telly being on, like a lot of old folk, I think my
grandparents still think the telly starts at 6 0'clock at night.
My Nana comes through with a cup of tea and a plate with a
Club biscuit and a Tunnocks tea cake on it. I check the Club,
it's no the one with the raisins in it, thank fuck. I take the
tea cake first and start reading the paper, the Record, which
is full of praise for the gallant Gers despite the fact the
cunts couldnae even score against CSKA in 90 minutes. I
just watched the game in the hoose as ah couldnae stand
tae watch it in company. I had watched their last home

game, against Brugges, in Martin's hoose, a rare occasion when we were the only two cunts there, and we sat there dejected as the cunts took an early lead. When Brugges equalised through we went fucking mental and Martin was on the phone to some hun cunt screaming "get it up ye!!!!" The hilarity continued until the The Huns scored the flukiest goal in European history and it was scored by a prick fae this area Scott Nisbett. They are actually trying to get the cunt in the Scotland team and he could barely get in the fucking school team. I read a bit aboot Celtic the morn, Charlie Nicholas is expected tae start, but the season is long gone. I'm almost finished my tea when I lift up the Club and there she is, majestic in her beauty, a crisp fiver, a nice pearl diver, that I sheepishly thank my Nana for. I go to the toilet and then tell her I'm off. I leave and my Grandad is talking tae another auld cunt so I nod but neither of them see me and ah head doon to shops at Pennywell before about turning and going to the ones at Groathill.

I head into the bookies and check the coupon for the morn. With that fiver and the pound from yesterday, plus the £30 Harry is subbing me tonight, that's a decent stash for the do the night. So I decide to bin the coupon and keep the dough. I walk back along Ferry Road and go into the phone boxes opposite Drylaw Polis and bell Martin at work whom I've just remembered was actually going with me to the Race Night anyway. As usual he picks up the phone immediately, a sure sign he's as busy as bar in Saudi Arabia. I inform him that Harry is now coming anaw now and his response is the predictable "Aw fur fucks sake". Martin is a Jambo but not one of the scum ones, whilst Harry is a Hibby and they go at it like cat and dug. After this, I head to the video shop at

Drylaw shops and scan to see if they've got anything good in but as usual they've no. I'm positive the cunts that work there keep aw the good stuff for themselves. I spy an Al Pacino one and scan the back to see that that cunt from Eastenders, Ricky, is in it, so I put it back and end up getting New Jack City, for the millionth time. I get over Ferry Road and head to the hoose and I can see the auld man is in so there is little chance of watching the video this efternin. Barry Norman Brian Dempsey is not. I shoot right up the stairs and lie on the bed and inevitably he's up behind me two minutes later, "We're gawn oot the night" I assume by "We" he means him and my Ma. I tell him I'm also gawn oot, tae the Race Night at the Swiss Cottage and you can tell he's raging aboot it. "Nae fucking singing up the road". I put on my crappy stereo and fire on a bit Ice Cube to chill oot the now. I borrowed his latest tape, The Predator, fae Martin last week and I'll copy it the day. I pick up 90 Minutes magazine and notice that they have predicted a 2-2 draw at Easter Road the morn, aye, maybe, but the season is fucked. Ah deek over at the wardrobe and wonder what I will wear the night, deciding on black shirt with grey fade that I bought aboot a month ago and black troosers and shoes. I head doonstairs and inform the old man I'll be taking a bath soon and he replies with a terse "Right". I head back up to get my stereo in the bathroom as soon as poss before he comes up and starts moaning, then I stick the immersion on and lie on my bed for a bit looking at my Celtic team photo and wondering if there will ever be a trophy at the front of it again. I go through and start running a bath as my auld man shouts up "Turn the immersion off now and don't have that radio on too loud and dinnae be in there too long!" Like a fucking prisoner of war camp in here. I like to run the bath before I switch the immersion off, keeping an eye out for the cunt coming up the stair. I get in and it's fucking piping hot and it takes me three sits to get ready when I realise I've forgot to turn the immersion off, so I get back oot and as I'm walking along the landing I hear my Ma coming in, like a search dog in a crack hoose she's on me right away with "You in that bath Sidney? Mind and turn the immersion off and don't make a mess in there" Bleak man.

All this grief has ruined the ambience of the bath fir me so I'm in and out in a few minutes, no even bothering tae pit the radio on. I dry myself then slip on a t shirt and pair of boxers, and clock the time, 4.46pm. Martin is getting the 32 bus at the bottom of Pennywell Road at 6.43 and I'm jumping on it at the top of Pennywell Road at 6.47 and then off up tae Corstorphine for the Race Night. Fuck knows how Harry is getting there. I flick on the portable, its auld and dying, and no even colour but works just and I start to get dressed, spraying myself with the Lynx Louise got me at Christmas. I think about Louise, she was awright but nipped yer heed and I was glad tae get rid in the end. Mind you this Lynx is coming in handy still. As usual I'm ready well early and so I go downstairs to see the sports headlines on the STV news at 6. As I walk in my auld man says "Where is it you're gawn again?" I tell him, again, it's the bus Race Night and he mumbles something aboot being a bit overdressed for Horse Racing, There's some pish coming up on the news aboot how going oot of Europe could be a good thing for The Huns but that's enough for me and I head out and decide to stroll along to the bus stop and a have a smoke til it comes. I'm that early that a 32 passes me and it's the one before the one I am due to get. I light up another fag and clock I've only got four left but Harry will have mair. The cunt never used tae smoke tae. I see the 32 come, the one that's mine and I jump on and see Martin sitting, back seat, lower deck. "Alright?" he says and I can tell something is up "I got sacked the day" what? what for? "Cunts said I didnae communicate enough" and as soon as he said it I knew that Martin was the type of cunt who could get sacked for that and it was also the only thing you could sack a cunt like Martin fir anaw. I asked him whit he was gonnae dae and he said "Git drunk" so I took that as my cue to drop it. Queensferry Road is rammed wi traffic and we crawl along there. Eventually we are on the Drum Brae and before long off for the Swiss Cottage. I see a couple of cunts from my bus heading in there and me and Martin head for the bar before taking our seats. Weird set up of wee alcove type seats and long tables. I scan the programme and can see loads of funny names on it. I was about to point some oot tae Martin when I saw a look of astonishment on his face, I was half expecting to turn round and see Harry behind me but no it was a bird fae the bus, Angie, and I wasn't sure why he looked like he did at her. "What you daeing here?" She says to him and now I was intrigued as he replied "Just here wi him" pointing at me. Fuck, what huv I done now? "Right, see ye later then" and she walked away. I was about to start powering the cunt about him potentially shagging her when he pipes up "That's the cow who sacked me the day". Christ almighty. Then this boy Lance appears with his bird and she sits next to me. Couple of the boys fae the bus raise eyebrows at this but I don't care.

The racing starts but by the fourth race it starts to get boring. I wish this cunt Harry would hurry the fuck up as I've done the six quid I had in. Thankfully at the interval he bounds in and sits doon "Awright boys?" Aye, fine. I wait a couple of seconds and ask him if he has that message and to be fair he comes across immediately. I can relax a bit noo. The rest of the night is spent bevvying and listening to Harry and Martin compare Hibs and Hearts teams. Yon Lance's bird winks at me from afar which is clocked by another one of the boys from the bus so I shout over that I got "*99 problems but a bitch ain't one*" which both tickles and confuses him. The disco is winding down and they inevitable You'll Never Walk Alone is played and cunts are using napkins as scarves. Even Martin joins in and that's a clear sign that, like me, he's pished. We bound out into the night and Harry and I light up fags. We walk up the Drum Brae towards the Rainbow but it's shut so we decide to wake every cunt up with a "No Huns in Munich" chant before grabbing a Taxi. I jump out at the top of Pennywell Road and gie Martin £3. Harry is asleep. I walk along Ferry Road singing "No Huns in Munich" all the way to the hoose which doesn't seem to disturb anyone apart from my auld man who upon me entering the hoose lets oot a "Get tae bed ya clown" so ah dae.

Players Lounge, Celtic Park, February 8th, 1994.

"Right guys, I've been sent here by the board to tell everyone that it's business as usual"

Paul McStay looked uncomfortable at Lou Macari's

utterances.

Susan handed round the big tin of Rover biscuits, much to the annoyance of Charlie Nicholas.

Peter Grant looked round the pennants that showed great games that Celtic had been involved in. How the fuck did it get to this.

"Now, the board have asked for anything positive to come out from you guys so in the next month or so I'll be promoting a young lad from the reserves"

Paul Byrne looked up, still half an eye on the Jaffa Cakes he hoped Susan would pass round after the Rover biscuits.

"So, let's stay positive guys, ok?"

With that, Lou left. The players sat there, like they were waiting to see the school headmaster, uncomfortable chairs in this tiny room. Someone had started making the pies.

Eventually, Charlie walked over to the Rover biscuits, it was empty now. "Business as usual? Aye, an empty fucking biscuit tin"

3

I wake the next day rough but no too bad. My plan is to slip
my clothes on and slip out the door. There is one
complication with that, hus the giro arrived? I slip my gear
on then I look from the top of the stairs and see that there
are three letters underneath the letterbox. The thing is the
auld man is up, I can hear him in the kitchen and it amazes
me that he's no picked them up. I creep doon the stairs, tip
toes all the way doon, and clock that two of the letters are
brown and one is white. Two giros I'm sure. I turn them
over and see B Dempsey on the first one and S Dempsey on
the second one. It crosses my mind to hide the auld man's
one but it's no worth the hassle. I slip mine into my pocket
and start turning the Yale lock. The auld man is frying
something so he can't hear it. I shut the door and crouch
past the windae until I am oot on the main street. Yes! I've
made it. Part two of my plan is shout up on Harry and then
hit the post office at Muirhoose shops. By rights my Giro
should be cashed at Drylaw Post Office but it was
something tae dae wi the Ferry Road, the main one, being a
boundary. "Sounds like the fucking River Ganges the wy
these cunts talk aboot it" my auld man always remarked
when he tried to change his post office to Drylaw. I was
feeling good about myself and went to check how much
hiries I hud pre Giro, I peeled off 17 bar which was no bad
and then it dawned on me, I'd forgot my fucking I.D. I was
faced with a Joseph Heller now, should I go back and get it
and risk the wrath of the auld man for singing last night or
try and blag my way oot of it at the post office but run the
risk of them no cashing it ataw? I decide to go back and
when I get in my auld man and Ma are in the lobby looking

at me "Where you been?" Eh, jist went for walk. "Do you know your giro didn't come?" Eh, naw. "Not been up tae anything huv ye?" The auld man has adopted his Taggart impression. No that I'm aware of, no. I did see a load of c... eh people having to cash theirs on Thursday after they'd no been sent oot like. Might be something like that. This seems to satisfy them and then my Ma ushers me intae the kitchen and asks if I'm going to the fitba the day. I hesitate until she gets her purse and slips me a tenner "Dinnae tell yer faither now" and I smile sheepishly calculating that I've now got 27 brick plus a giro to cash so that means I'll no feel the hit of the 30 bar I'll be gieing back tae Harry. Oh I've been flying... Mama, there ain't no denying. I nip upstairs pretending to go to the toilet and grab my National Insurance card for I.D. I nip back doon and shout cherrio, nipping oot before anyone can reply. I'm late for Harry and bolt doon the road and amazingly the cunt is at his stair, smoking a fag. I pass him 25 nicker and he looks at me suspiciously, I await him telling me that it was actually 30 I borrowed when he says "25 back awready like? Did you buy any drink last night ya cunt?" I shrug and we hit the post office and as usual there is a queue and as usual the big lassie wi ginger hair and her bairn wi her is in front of me. She must sign on in Duke Street as I've no seen her at High Riggs. I get to the front, hand the giro over and typically, no one asks for I.D. I find this set up mental, they send you a giro through the post only for you to immediately take it back to the post office. Surely we could cut oot the middle man there? No matter, I get oot there sharpish and Harry asks what the rush is, and I tell him I don't want to bump into my faither and we head doon for a number 16 but Harry says we should get a pint in The

Gunner first and a game of pool. So we do. I beat him 2-1 in games and we have the two pints. It looks like half my street is in the pub and it was only 10 past 9 in the morning when we arrived. Harry is feeling flush and we get a taxi at the Triangle Club and shoot doon to Elm Row in it. I'm pretty chuffed wi this until Harry says "You jist get this wi that fiver ye owe me aye?" I can hardly refuse I suppose although by the time we get to Elm Row it actually cost £5.60 so that's an extra greyhound right away cause of the taxi cunt's tip. Harry has already bounded out the taxi and is shouting up to cunts outside the Elm Bar that Pearces opens at 11, no half past like the Elm bar so they aw come doon as if some cunt has just shot a starter gun. We meet a boy fae the bus and all have a Guinness, the boy fae the bus is a wideo from Granton and immediately hits me with "Here, you couping that Lance's burd or what?" I smile and Harry says "What's this?" but I blank the pair of them. In all honesty I'm still half cut from last night and this Guinness is making me feel a bit queasy. We decant and head for the Elm Bar as that's where we are getting the tickets. Harry has his awready like. By One-O we are aw scooping like fuck and I've had about eight becks and six vodka and cokes. Just then that Lance comes in with his burd and aw eyes are on me, bar his. He greets me like a long lost brother which confuses every cunt, none more than me. His bird sits right next to me and a couple of drinks later she quite clearly grabs my arse as I head to go to the toilet. Thing is I'm now so drunk I don't care. We leave the boozer and although it's no a long walk along Montgomery Street to the ground it feels like it when you're as gaga'd as we are.

The sun is shining but I feel fucked, cunts are talking to me and in high spirits but I wish I could just go to a toilet and collapse. We move onto Easter Road and Middleton's looks rammed. Harry keeps on going doon to go to the Hibs end, normally I'd meet him efter the game but the cunt is going to Fife efter and so I'll probably just head hame. Over the Bothwell Bridge and the sun is annoying as fuck in my eyes, and I see the ground proper for the first time. Up tae the Dunbar end, in, and up the hill and onto the terracing just as the teams come out. Charlie Nicholas is starting. A guy next to me passes me a half bottle of Vodka and I take a big swig, which makes me want tae be sick. No as much as Celtic though, 3-0 down at half time and cunts are going bananas and one boy fae my bus has lost it, in a state of anger and tears. The wideo fae Granton, that I'm wi, is threatening to kill the entire Hibs end until a polis has enough and lifts him. I follow him to the bit of the Dunbar end next to the main stand and hear the polis say to him "If I hud my way ya weegie cunt, I'd stand you there for 90 minutes so you could watch yer team get fucked" This enrages the wideo who replies "I'm fae Edinburgh ya fascist bastard" and with that, he's huckled.

I look back and can't take any mair, I ask to be let oot and make it back to the Elm Bar where by the look of it half the bus huvnae even left. I take one drink but slip oot as I'm totally fucked, jumping on a 16 at the top of the walk. I get off at the bottom of Pennywell Road and hike it up to the top before getting tae the hoose and crashing oot just efter I found oot that Charlie Nicholas had pulled one back for us but we still got beat 3-1.

4

I had to be up early the next morning as I was playing fitba
at Saughton astro turf. I totally regretted it now of course
and it was compounded by the fact that it's a hard place tae
get tae. It was a waste of time as well as we got well beat
and hardly any cunt tried. I took a number 1 hame and
went tae bed.

I didn't feel back to normal until a few days later. I got up
this morning and the news was full of a guy called Stephen
Lawrence being stabbed near his hoose. Christ can ye
imagine that? I always feel safe near ma hoose, I ken
everybody aroond here and don't think there's anyone who
would want to stab me. I certainly dinnae want tae stab
anyone either. I hope they get the bastard who did it.

5

My auld man is asking me what time I'm gawn tae sign on at. Hardly seems like two weeks since I did but it is and I'm aboot tell him when I hear the postie and see on inspection see that there is a letter for me with an American stamp on it. I open it up

Ferris Moran
647 S. Passyunk Ave
Philadelphia, Pa 19147

Dear Sidney,
    I just turned 20 myself but it's a pretty lousy birthday as I can't legally drink until I'm 21 (not that it stops me though). I heard you can drink in Britain when you're 18, that's so cool. I'm working for my uncle right now fixing cars which is good money but I'm hoping to go to college soon, maybe at St Josephs university. My favorite band is Pearl Jam but my old man is an Elvis fan too, I guess that's universal. My favorite movie is Jurassic park. I took a girl to see it last year in the theatre and it was scary as hell. Celtic, huh? Are they related to the Boston Celtics? Cause I hate them. They used to beat my Philadelphia Sixers all the time and I'll never forgive Larry Bird. We don't have any soccer teams here except for the indoor soccer league team, the Kixx. But nobody goes to those games.

Catch ya later,
Ferris

I read it twice and felt quite chuffed aboot it. Although, obviously, I'll need to put the boy right aboot Celtic. I'll no show it tae my auld man either as he will crack up with the cunt fir saying that and probably want to knock fuck oot ae the boy. Which wouldnae be fair on the boy as he wouldnae ken whit fur.

Funny name that anaw, Ferris. There's a boy here, Paul Ferris, who is always in the paper but Ferris is this boy's first name. The only Ferris I know is that boy Ferris Bueller from that film. Good film that, I love that bit where he is singing in New York or something, naw Chicago, and he's like "I recall, CENTRAL PARK IN FALL!!!" and this reminiscing leads the auld man tae shout fae the living room "Rap up you, av telt ye aboot that singing, fucking woke the whole street up a fortnight ago with it" That makes ma mind up, I'm no gawn up tae sign on wi the cunt. I nip up early and it's empty in the brew, the boy just signs me on and lets me go. Amazingly I've still got seven bar on me and so I head doon tae Virgin and HMV to see if there's any good tapes or videos on sale. It's one of those horrible days where it's hot but no sunny and I take my jaiket off and put it over my shoulder then just carry it as that's whit my auld man does wi the over the shoulder thing. I cross at the west end and start motoring tae Virgin first. I'll check the videos as I've no seen a decent one in ages and I've watched aw the ones Martin lent me. I pick up Reservoir Dogs. I kept meaning tae see it but never hud. I was looking at the back of it, aw the guys dressed like they are going tae a funeral when she started talking tae me "It's good that, I saw it in the Cameo" I look up , then to my right and there's a lassie standing there, looks aboot the same age as me but a wee bit smaller. All I can think is "where the fuck is the Cameo". I look at her and tell her that I've always fancied it. "That's no way take talk aboot a lady" she says sternly, I fluster a bit and apologise but then she says "Am only kidding ye" Her accent is funny, no Edinburgh. "My name is Heny, but my friends call me Honey, it's a nickname" Right, Honey aye, nice name, kindae makes me want mine to be "Bee". She looks at me for a bit then punches my shoulder and says "You're funny". She's wearing jeans and a t shirt and looks gorgeous, olive skin that's glowing and long brown hair. So eh, where dae ye come from then? "Jordanhill" she replies and I huvnae a clue where that is and she realises that and adds "That's in Glasgow by the way". Right, aye, Glasgow, I'm through there a lot fir the fitba like. "Oh football, I'm still thinking about whether to like that or not" So what brings you through tae Edinburgh then? "Well I'm looking at Universities, it's between Edinburgh, obviously, or Strathclyde. If I pick Edinburgh, you'll be able to show me around eh?" and she punches my shoulder again. Eh aye, nae bother. "So, you going to buy that Video then?" Video? What vid, oh aye, eh aye I think so. "It's just that I have it at home and could lend you it if you like? Or you could come through when you go to the football?" Aye, eh, jist thit the fitba is finished the noo and, actually..., wait a minute..., I'm gonnae be through on June 1st for a thing, it's no really a game like it's just a thing they've put on cause The H, eh Rangers stood in The Jungle and eh, I'm confusing her, eh, June 1st "Splendid, that's a date then, I'll meet you at the train station, I've got a card here with my phone number on, take that and ring me next week, oh, what's your name by the way?" Eh, Sid. "Nice, ok Sid, speaking of train stations, I must get to one now, nice talking to you". And like that, she was gone. I tried to play the cool one but inside burds were singing.

Boardroom, Celtic Park, Glasgow, February 24th 1994

"Right, now I know we have the issue with the Ibrox tickets, let me tell you, that's Murray blowing out his arse because they are seating the East Enclosure at Ibrox and the stupid bastard forgot that he had nowhere to put the fans from there, so he's made an issue out of a few broken seats. Listen, we don't want to go there anyway and the fans won't want to either. Also I've told Lou to bring in a player from the reserves, give the fans something to look forward to"

Michael Kelly was in bullish mood.

"Eh?"

"Tom, it's that simple. Now, as I said a few weeks ago, we have something big, David and I have been working on this for a while, Chris has had an input too, we have secured the funding for Cambuslang. Gefinor will provide it, Patrick Nally has flown in from New York and we are doing a press conference tomorrow, Kevin will front it but I want us all there"

A stunned silence went across the boardroom.

Jack McGinn looked at the photo of Sir Robert Kelly

"Michael, eh, what are the details, how much will it cost, is

this based on the plan of 1992?"

"To a point Jack, yes. The capacity will be 40,000, we feel this is adequate given our recent attendances"

"Can you show me the signed contracts?"

"Och Tom, let's not get bogged down in that nonsense, this is a great day for Celtic"

"Michael, you show me the contracts or the letters of guarantee or I won't be at any fucking press conference"

And with that, Tom Grant got up to leave.

"I'm with Tom" and Jack McGinn shuffled out as well.

Silence again in the room as eyes fixed on Jimmy Farrell

"Is that lunch?"

6

I sat doon the next day to write back to that boy Ferris.

Dear Ferris,

Thanks for writing back to me mate. First I better tell ye that my team Celtic has nout to do with the Boston Celtics. Our best player is a guy called Paul McStay. We are no doing very well at the minute as we seem to have no money. i should tell tell ye but I met a lassie yesterday, get this, her name is "Honey". Don't think I've ever met anyone called that before. Anyway she invited me through tae her hoose in Glesgae to watch a film, Reservoir Dogs, have you seen it? And do you have a girlfriend? Also what shows do you watch on the TV? I like fitba programmes and a programmed called Minder which is aboot a boy who batters folk for his boss who makes money.

Yours
Sid

I'll post it on Saturday when I cash my giro. I wonder when tae phone Honey, I only met her yesterday, is it too soon? Mind you, there's nae cunt in, perfect time tae phone as I'd hate the auld man lugging in. This is fucking bleak man. I look at her number, check the time, 3.03pm, fuck it, I'll phone. I dial the number and it rings for a while then a lassies voice answers really loudly, I say her name and there are giggles, then I hear the receiver being grabbed and a mair familiar voice answers "Hello?" Eh Hi, Honey? It's Sidney from Edinburgh? "Oh, Sidney, how are you?" Eh, fine, jist thought I'd phone and arrange that da, eh, time to come see ye. "Right yes, um, well, what's today?" Eh, Friday. "Right, well, what about Sunday?" Sunday is good for me although a couple of weeks before I'd be in Glesgae again but fuck it, Aye that's fine. "So, will you be driving through?" Eh naw, the train I'd say. "Ok, I'll come meet you at Queen St station, say two o'clock?" Aye that's fine, see ye then, bye "Bye!" Fucking Betty Windsor St. The only time I've ever been there is to go to Hampden for Scotland games. I assume she will know the score but I better phone up and check the times of trains anyway. Right, there's yin that gets me in at 1.54pm which is ideal.

At that the auld man comes in and looks at me suspiciously "Alright?" Aye. "Whit ye been daeing the day then?" Eh, nout much. "Right listen, I'm working the weekend, Dougie says ye can work tae, £20 a shift" Eh, a cannie on Sunday. "Fuck ye oan aboot?" Am gawn tae see somebody, "Fur fucks sake, when?" Two o'clock. "Two o'clock, we'll be done by then" Eh, when will a get paid? "When you've done the fucking joab to satisfactory levels" and he fucked off into the kitchen after that. I suppose it wisnae bad, 40 bar in my tail and I widnae be watching the Scottish Cup final anyway wi they cunts in it but I wanted to have ma heed cleared for gawn tae Glesgae and now ma auld man is gonnae be nipping it aw weekend. Fucks sake.

The shifts worked oot no bad. Dougie, the boy ma auld man works wi, is no a bad cunt really. At break time we were having sandwiches ma maw had made and Dougie gave me a Trio biscuit. I jist finished it when he says "right, come on youse, what dae ye think this is, a fucking holiday camp?"

then he winked at me. We finished at quarter past 12 on the Sunday which coincidentally was fifteen minutes before the boozers opened. We were working up at Barnton painting these big hooses white wi black trim. Efter I finished I got a 41 up the toon and was up there for 12.50pm as the roads were quiet wi it being a Sunday. I saw this hun walking towards me and it reminded me they beat Aberdeen yesterday tae win the treble. I knew fuck all else aboot it as my auld man would never buy a paper efter them daeing something like that. It was a nice day and I got washed in the station for a couple of minutes and then made the 1pm train. I kept feeling the 40 bar in my pocket and it felt good. I left my Giro money in the hoose as I'd vowed to start saving up noo that that the fitba was finished. It wisnae bad for the fare either, £3, thank fuck they dinnae have they barriers here like they dae in London or I'd have never have made the train.

As we leave Croy, my stomach starts churning and in all honesty I started regretting daeing this. I heard that Clyde are gonnae move tae Croy, fuck knows why, there's nout there. The train seems to be crawling intae Glesgae, past Cowlairs, Cowlairs, rings a bell that, cannie think why. We pass under a tunnel and the guard announces that it's the last stop. This is it. We crawl intae the platform and I start needing a shite, fucking bleak. It's probably nerves. Eventually it stops and I get off, letting a women whose two bairns have screamed aw the way fae Falkirk get off afore me. I walk down the platform and scan around, nae cunt ootside the bar, cannie see any cunt ootside Burger King either. Fucks sake man. I'm really bursting now but I dinnae want tae fuck off and then she thinks I've no came. Mind

you, she's no here yit and the carsey is just over there. I bolt
over and pay the robbing cunts their 10p. It's a fucking long
corridor but there's a trap open and I dive in, bolt the door
after the second attempt and git my troosers doon quick.
The release is refreshing and then there's a mini explosion.
I clean up as much as I can off my arse and use about 40
sheets. I came in and got undressed so quick that my
troosers were sort of wrapped round my boxers and I need
to unfold them a bit before putting my belt on again. I walk
out fast but then about turn to wash my hands, get out this
time and there's still no sign of her. At this point I've nae
idea what tae dae. I've got her number here but if she's oan
her way then there's no much point in phoning it and then
if I phone her and she's there, I'm sunk. A boy brushes past
me and I realise that I've no moved far enough away from
the toilet entrance so I step forward a wee bit, still
wondering what the fuck tae dae. Then two hands go on my
eyes and I fucking shit myself, not literally as there's fuck
all left in the guts anyway and I turn quickly to see her
"Hello!, Am I late? Sorry, I got a cab down" She came in fae
the taxi rank side, I wisnae expecting that. Still, whatever
else is said or whatever else happens, she's turned up. That
hus tae be a good thing.

7

Her hoose looks massive. In fact, it's aboot the same size as ma hoose and the yins either side of it as well. As oor taxi pulls up I tell her I'll get it and she doesn't bat an eyelid. I volunteered as it was only £2.75 which I could hardly believe. Would have been double that in Edinburgh. I gie the boy the £3 and he pretends to gie me change but I wave it away and he has a "Job done" expression aboot him. Her front door is already open and that makes me assume that her Ma and Dad must be in but there's nae cunt tae be seen. Her living room looks like Habitat's front windae. She lives in place called Jordanhill which makes me think of Celtic's assistant manager. She tells me to sit doon and so I dae and she goes through the kitchen and brings back two chilled bottles of Becks. She sits doon and looks at me and says "So what is it you do?" I tell her that I'm unemployed but I was daeing a couple of shifts with my auld man and Dougie this weekend and she smiles "Manual Labour" I'm no sure what this means but tell her if she means paid fae the neck doon then she's right and she laughs. I neck the Becks and she asks if I want to put the video on and I agree. She's hardly touched her Becks which makes me feel I drank mine too quick but she brings me another one all the same. She sticks the video on and we watch the trailers, which are pish, and then it starts. Martin always reckons ye can tell a good film by its trailers so if his theory is correct, this will be utter garbage. I scan roond the room and see no traces of any fitba affinity anywhere. There's a photie of Honey on the wall with what looks like her Ma and Dad and her Ma is black. There's loads of stuff around the house that looks really modern. Honey says "I've put some Meatballs on for us, hope that's ok, bit of a tradition here" Eh, aye. She sits on a big couch whilst I'm on a chair. This film is fucking barry although unlike anything I've ever seen before. The boy fae Mean Streets is in it, no Johnny Boy, the other one, but I don't recognise any cunt else. Honey looks over at me now and again and smiles. She pauses the film and goes to get the Meatballs. They are small and I've got 24 on my plate, with some chips. They taste good although fuck all like the ones my Ma makes. I tell her they are good and she smiles and sort of hunches her shoulders a bit. It's now I realise that I really fancy her. There's a scene in the film where this polis gets his ear sliced off and Honey lifts the cushion above her face when it happens, I laugh when she does it and almost put my right foot on my now empty plate.

After the film she tells me that her Ma and Dad will be in about eight. I take this as my cue to leave but she asks me where I am going? "Oh, Sorry, I didn't mean for you to leave! I meant, oh, it's ok" I'm unsure what she means by this and I'm sure I've upset her. Then I remember something Dougie says to me yesterday "Nivir lit a bird know yer interested until she makes it clear she wants it" I think about this and move over tae the couch. She asks me what I am daeing and I tell her that I'm hoping tae kiss her and she blushes, then I bag off with her on her couch and it was fucking barry. We separate but keep looking at each other and she says "look, you better go" Aye, nae bother. I compose myself and see the time, 6.05pm, I should get the 7 o'clock train. There's something wrong with her though, I can tell. As we get to the door she says "Look, I really like you Sidney, do you like me?" Aye, of course ah dae. "It's just that, well, I don't know what to say, it's, oh God, this is horrible" What the fuck is wrong with her. We are standing in her lobby and my heart is going ten tae the dozen. "Ok, it's just that, I sort of had a boyfriend and we just broke up, well, he wasn't really a boyfriend, we went out a few times, some nice restaurants and one day he drove me up to Gleneagles and he's a bit older than me" I want to kill the cunt. "And it was ok, but he was a bit, sort of, full on, all flash and undignified and he basically won't leave me alone, he writes letters to me a lot and he comes round asking for me" My mate Ferris writes to me but he's a sound cunt "and it's just, I don't know how to tell him it's over" I tell her it's ok, I understand and that she had a life before she met me, which is none of my business and I am not going to start any bother because of this and this makes her smile "Thanks, thanks so much, I was really dreading him coming round when you were here and starting some kind of scene as he thinks he can do what he wants, when he wants, just because he has money" Hey, don't worry about, I finger the 35 bar in my tail, I'm cool with it. She smiles and gies me a cuddle and then we kiss again. I feel like I'm on MDMA with that kiss and could skip to the fucking train station if truth be told. We kiss once more and I move off in search of a taxi, she stands at her door, arms folded, watching me. I think I love her. I walk a couple of steps then turn back to her "By the way, what fitba team does he support?"

"Um, Rangers? yeah Rangers"

Bleak, man. Bleak man.

Press Conference, Celtic Park, February 25th, 1994.

"Good morning gentlemen. We called you here today to announce the fact that we have secured the funding for our new stadium project at Cambuslang. Now, you know Michael Kelly, the other gentleman beside me is Patrick Nally from Stadivarious. His company will oversee the project and it is they who helped secure the funds."

Cameras clicked and journalists scribbled.

"Questions?"

"Yes David, can you tell me the sums of money involved here?"

"Of course, the initial funding, already secured, is for twenty million pounds"

Patrick Nally shuffled in his seat.

At the back of the room, out of sight of everyone, Tom Grant and Jack McGinn watched in disbelief as this web of lies was woven.

"Jack, this is going to kill us, you know that don't you?"

"Yes, but what can we do?"

"Call Fergus"

8

I wake up the next day, it's a Monday, but there is no gloom. Yesterday was one of the best days of my life and I stick my stereo on, pumping up Ice Cube "*I got a Mack 10 for Officer Wind, damn his devil ass needs to be shipped back to Kansas, in a casket, cool cut faggot, now he ain't nothing but food for the maggots*" This makes me think of this hun cunt Honey talked to me about. I am truly fucking sick of these bastards. A treble, four years of nothing for Celtic and now, this? I should tell the auld man as he'd probably batter fuck oot the cunt on principle alone but I'm no involving him as he will just gie me hassle aboot Honey. From her name, onwards. This hun cunt again is in my mind, on my mind

"To get some respect we had to tear this muthafucka up"

I slip doonstairs and my auld man is sitting with a paper that looks like the Weekly News fae Friday. "Aye, aye, it's Warren Beatty, how did it go yesterday?" Eh, aye, fine. I've no idea who Warren Beatty is. I go ben the kitchen and make myself some Sugar Puffs as there is nae Coco Pops left. I really cannie stand Sugar Puffs mind. The packet is blue and red and yellow and there's a bear on it. Bear. Teddy Bears. Huns. That hun cunt. Fucks sake.

"You had to get Rodney to stop me"

I bin most of the puffs and head back up the stair. Then I remember, fuck me, I've no cashed my giro yit. I get ma troosers and socks on, fuck it I'll wear the same boxers again, and put that hooded top on my Auntie in America sent me. I bail oot and leave the £30 I have in my pocket on the mantle piece for ma digs and I'll gie my Ma that tenner I owe her oot ma giro when I get back. I slip doon the post office and the queue is longer than ever. It's aw cunts cashing their Monday books so The Gunner will be doing a roaring trade shortly. I pit ma I.D. doon, no checked as usual, and she hands over the notes. I make ma way back tae the hoose via Crawfords at Drylaw Shops where I get two sliced sausage rolls and a pineapple cake. I get the auld man two pies. I get back via the new traffic lights on Ferry Road and when I get in I tell the auld man I got him two pies to which he replies "Fucking hell, two days graft and he's spending like Imelda Marcos"

It doesnae pay to be nice in this fucking hoose.

I'm halfway up the stairs wi ma scran when the auld man shouts me back. I double back but leave the scran on the stairs as the dug is asleep in the living room. I ask what is it and she says "Some lassie was on the phone for you, then, aboot five minutes later, a boy" My hearts skips, eh, who was the lassie? "Fuck am I? a mind-reader? She says tae phone her, ye huv her number" Must be Honey. I go to walk oot and he says "Whit aboot the other message?" What other message? "The boy, he left a number, Glesage one" and my auld man hands me it on a pink Harrowers bookie slip. It says on it "Findlay" and then it hus a Glesage number on it. I've nae clue who this is but I'll gie him a phone. Efter I've phoned Honey. I go to the lobby and dial her number. It's one of they answer machines so I dinnae leave a message. I then phone this other number and strange voice answers "Hello? Hello?" Aye this is Sidney, you phoned me?

"Ah yes, Sidney, this would be the shyster going after my Princess eh? Well, this is a piece of friendly advice Sidney, you go near my Heny again and I will roll right over the top of you, got it? You're nothing, you're less than nothing, people like you don't exist, you can't beat me, I will outspend you at every opportunity, I am the future". I am stunned by this, I don't know what to say so he goes on "Heny and I will be all over Europe soon, where will you be, eh? eh? I'll tell you where, nowhere. Heny tells me you're on the up? Pah, a pig just flew by my window, stay away from her" and he slammed the phone doon.

I walk upstairs and grab my rolls and cake, shit, forgot the drink. I go downstairs and dilute some Willie Lows juice and head back up. By now the sliced sausage is cauld but I scran it anyway.

I lie back on my bed and think. The boy, Findlay? Fucking bleak man. First bird in a while and some bam is on the phone it me awready. Bleak. I flip over the tape and it's that bit on The Predator where Ice Cube is being interviewed so I fast forward it. It goes past the bit I want so I rewind a wee bit then a wee bit mair.

"You can't trust a big butt and a smile, no that's the old style"

Honey doesnae have a big erse though. Well, unless you count Findlay.

First Team and Reserve Team training sessions, Barrowfield, February 25th, 1994.

"Dddid you see that ggoal from Brazil on the ttelly last night?" Brian O'Neil had the attention of Simon Donnelly.

"The gguy rolled the defender hit it like a pppitching wwwwedge, but with power, was unreal"

"I could do that no problem" replied Donnelly

"fffuuu, go on then"

Donnelly grabbed a couple of balls and lined them up. The first team had finished their session, no one was around. There wasn't even anyone looking in from the Celtic Supporters Assoc. He stood with his back to goal, O'Neil behind him. As described, he rolled O'Neil and smashed it in the top corner of the goal but with that back lift they had spoken about. As he was about tell O'Neil "That's how to do it", Donnelly heard a voice.

"Could you do that again son?"

Standing in front of him was only the first team manager, Lou Macari.

"Eh, aye, I think so"

Macari looked at him as if to say "Well, go on then"

Donnelly obliged and repeated the action beautifully.

Macari smiled and, as he walked away, said "Thanks"

9

I crashed oot on ma bed aw efternin and woke up to the phone ringing. I realised there was no one in and ran doon tae answer it. It was Honey. "Sidney? Thank God, listen I'm sorry about earlier, that cretin came round my house and forced his way in, just barged past me and saw your number, so I told him you were my pal from Edinburgh and he just flipped out, what did he say to say you?" Eh, nothing really, just that you were his bi, eh girlfriend "No, I'm not, honestly, oh God what a prick he really is" This was the first time I'd heard her swear and even then it was just prick. "Listen, you said you'd be in Glasgow in June?" Aye, June 1st "Good, can we meet then, please, I want to see you" Aye, well it will need to be during the day like as I'm gawn tae The Blow Away The Blues pairty like. "Fine, no bother" Unless, like, ye want tae come wi me?" "Yeah, of course, what time you coming through" Well I suppose I could get through for eh, 2 o'clock? "Great, sounds great, and again, I'm so sorry about that utter moron, please don't hate me" No, I won't, ok, see you later then "Bye Sidney".

Christ, some amount of grief for one bag off.

I belled my mate Chas after that, he was meant to be coming wi me to The Blow Away The Blues, and when I told him I'd be meeting a bird first he was very supportive "Ah fur fucks sake ya cunt, this is aboot blowing the huns away, I was up at the Priest last Sunday getting holy water and everything, whit the fuck ye wanting to bring a bird fir? Is she a Tim?"

June 1st was the blowing away the blues party, I'd better hud oan tae the giro money until then but fancied a few pints in the Ferryboart the day. I slipped up there and was told by a mate of my auld man's that he'd just left him in The Doocot. Then I saw this big hun Bobby who started slagging me and when I telt him we'd be back soon he replied "Ach ye've been saying that since ye hud plenty hair at the front". I encounter a lot of cunts like this but deep doon Bobby is no bad, his auld man is right bigot though. I mind one time he won a raffle in The Gunner and the prize was a signed Hibs top. Every cunt was laughing at him winning it until he took it outside and burnt it. That's mental. One time me and my mate blagged our way intae this do where they were gieing away free Celtic and Huns tops. I took the Hun tops for the lassie at my work at the time and she was over the moon. I saw a boy, Goose, at the bar, he's an awright gadgie like and funny as fuck. He was shouting this cunt George's name who was sitting over the other side of the bar and then every time he looked up Goose would act as if nothing had happened and it was driving this cunt George loopy. That's just Goose like. So I hud a wee scoop wi him when this Irish boy started talking tae us. In all honesty I fucking hate it when someone just interrupts your conversation just because they can hear what you are saying. Bleak man. Anyway this boy starts talking about this post office and how he is going to rob it. I've encountered many cunts like him before and the usual way to deal with them is to nod, smile and then hope you never see them again. Then though this cunt asks me and Goose if we want in. He'd dae aw the heavy work, we'd be there for show and to ensure no cunt fucked with us. Goose looked at him and goes "We talking shooters here?" and the boy says we wouldn't need them. He quoted a couple of names at Goose which impressed him but in all honesty I just wanted to get the fuck oot of there. This wasn't my scene and although I'd love the money, I'm no criminal. I did once have to pay the brew money back they said they'd overpaid me but I'm no *that* desperate for cash. Goose scooped up and told the cunt he would sleep on it and then I telt him I was gawn fir fags but I did a B1 and went hame. When I got in, my auld man said there was another call from a guy and I'd just missed it. Fucks sake, I bet it is that Hun cunt again at it. I'm sick of this shit. I went up tae ma room and thought about it a bit, I love Honey, she's barry but this is all daeing ma heed in. Still, I cannie gie in, not to a Hun. I was aboot tae pit on some music when the phone rang again. Fucking hell man. My auld man shouted for me tae git it as he was in the living room sleeping off the bevvy, no that he telt me that, I jist surmised it. I was going tae gie this bastard and earfay and when I picked up I was ready then confused. "Sid?" Aye, "It's Goose, listen, fuck that daft cunt in the battle crusier, I'll huv him Scotland by the morn, see you doon the boom boom at one o" Then he pit the phone doon. I ey knew Goose was an awright gadgie.

Manager's office, Celtic Park, February 26th

"Come in, son"

Simon Donnelly nervously walked in and shut the door behind him.

"I'm going to be starting you in the next couple of weeks, once all this boycott nonsense has gone away. Hopefully that

will die with the game being off today"

Lou smiled.

10

Incredibly, av managed to keep £35 for the day in Glesgae.
It's pishing doon in Edinburgh when I meet Chas and head
through on the train. Aw the way he is quizzing me aboot
Honey but I bat most of it away. So he goes onto Celtic "Dae
ye think any of the first team will be there the night? Av got
ma doubts like, my big brar told me Paul McStay is away tae
Italy oan holiday" I ponder this "That cunt Brady better no
be there anyway, he's fucked us up fir good" Ah don't know
like "Aye he hus" I'm no sure, that game at Ibrox in January,
the yin that wanker Trevor Steven scored wi a heeder, we
played them off the fucking park that day. "Aye and what
did that cunt Brady dae? Fucking conceded the league.
Conceded the fucking league in January, you dinnae dae
that man, no it Celtic, no matter how bad things git" I think
about this and Chas is right, he should never have done that
but we did stop their unbeaten run in March there and that
wis the night my auld man and my auntie were up dancing
at that do we were aw it and they banged right intae the
disco and the whole thing smashed. Brady was the manager
that day and Collins was exceptional but it wis the front
two of Payton and McAvennie who ran the Huns ragged.
"Aye, that wis a good day right enough"

My mind starts to wander to Honey as the train speeds up
again past Falkirk High. I realise that I've missed her. I get a
wee butterflies feeling and think I am taking a beamer but
Chas hasn't noticed anything, he's looking at something in
the Daily Record "Here, huv ye seen this? A player has been
charged with going with rent boys" He hands me the paper
over the table and I scan the article and it says an unnamed

international fitba player, has his age as 31 and says he plays in Scotland. We both ponder this and I come up with Packie Bonner, thinking of his age n that but Chas explodes. "Whit, get tae fuck, no Packie, he's a fucking God. And he's married anaw" We both think about this and then my mind wanders to Honey again, she's meeting me at the station after the game. She was going to go but that cunt Chas being here as well was too bleak man. I'll phone her from the station though. We ease through Cowlairs, slow as fuck as usual, and eventually get in. I breeze for the phone boxes as Chas heads for WH Smith for fags. I bell Honey and it rings for ages, then her auld man's answering machine comes on so I leave a message saying I will meet her at the station at 10 o'clock. I omit the fact that we have got a hotel for the night. It was her idea, said we could have space to talk, and I was delighted but I'd need to be back in Edinburgh at some point the morn to sign on.

Chas bolts out the shop and his usual style lights up two fags then hands me one. Almost immediately a train boy coughs and points behind us at a No Smoking sign "That's a bad cough you've got there" Chas says to the boy without bothering to look at the sign. "I was referring to the No Smoking sign behind you" We both look at it and Chas retorts to the boy "Aye, it's a belter pal" and points behind the boy and the boy says "What is it?" So Chas says "I was referring to that Boots sign there pal, best place to go for a cough remedy" and with that we head for a taxi.

We tell the driver "Gallowgate" and start up a conversation about this rent boys thing again. As we both sat there thinking about it, the driver looks in his mirror and says

"Do you no know who it is naw? It's Charles Bough" and we both sit back in our seats to take this in. Chas speaks first "Speaks fucking volumes" and we get dropped off at Bairds. It's no too busy and, as usual, our necks hurt after being in there for a few minutes but it's worth it. Bertie Auld is behind the bar and in great form. We are necking Buds as they've nae Becks. The war songs are blasting and I'm feeling fucking barry again. I think about Honey and get a nice glow which has Chas worried "Fuck's wrong wi you ya cunt?" I tell him I'm looking forward to the night and that seems to appease him. Then a blast from the past comes on, Madness by Madness. Everyone in the bar goes mental, pure Nutty Boys, pure Celtic. See that's the thing aboot Celtic, only Celtic could organise a daft kickaboot and huv cunts like me and Chas come through fae Edinburgh to go to it. After the season we huv hud, those cunts winning the treble n that, here we aw ur aw jumping aboot like mad men. Especially Chas.

"Propaaaagandaaa ministers, PROPAGANDA MINISTERS!!!!"'" and he jumps on my back and I lurch forward and my Bud half spills but no cunt cares. Fucking barry.

Efter that we started cracking tae this boy called Kev fae Kings Park in Glesgae. He was sound, funny as fuck although we were slagging his slick back do. He telt us that the hoose he is noo in once belonged tae Jock Stein. It sounded believable and we both, me and Chas, wished we had a camera wi us.

We make our way along the Gallowgate and it's still pishing

doon. That makes us think they will be toiling for a crowd the night, but as long as there's a few hundred of us singing in The Jungle, that's aw that matters. Thing is, when we get there, aboot an hour before kick off, there's already thousands queuing to get in. I grab a programme which says that Dukla Pumpherston will play a selection of Coronation Street, Eastenders and Casualty stars and then The Lisbon Lions will play Man Utd 1968. So it is a fucking kickaboot.

We queue up and get in. Thankfully. See the last game of the season, against Dundee, I queued to get in and they shut the turnstile just before I was going in. This cunt Bobby got in before me, and he'd just appeared on the bus. The thing is, although he is a Tim, he's also a fucking Killie fan and when he got photographed as the last cunt in The Jungle, he was wearing a fucking Killie top under his jumper. Stupid bastard, that's probably why they organised this.

It's clear that despite the cunts advertising for a few hundred Tims to come along and stand in The Jungle and blow away the blues, there are fucking thousands here. So many in fact that they have had to open the Celtic end. Fucking unbelievable and Chas, by now completely nuggets, is in tears. "I cannie take this man, what a fucking support, when are we gonnae put these orange bastards in their place pal, when? I'm sick of it, no matter what we dae, they seem to dae it better the noo, I fucking hate them"

Me tae.

Living room of Michael Kelly, February 26th, 1994.

"That's right aye, frozen pitch"

"What? I don't care about Love Street, St Mirren have nothing to do with Celtic"

"We are letting the media know at 11am"

"hahaha, aye, let's see what they do with their pathetic boycott now"

"Cheers Gerry, what's that? Of course, no problem at all Mr McSherry"

Michael Kelly put the phone down.

11

I get up the next day a bit groggy, at the bottom of ma bed is a letter. I see the post mark and it's fae Ferris. I flip on my stereo and blast oot Kashmir by Led Zeppelin, which always make me feel fucking barry. I open up the letter and see, fir the first time, that it's handwritten.

Hey pal, Paul McStay? I wonder if he's related to my Dads friend Jim McStay. He's Irish as they come. I hear ya about your team not having any money. My football team is the Philadelphia Eagles and our owner is a cheapskate. I hope he sells them soon. We need new uniforms too. Don't get me wrong I love our colors, green and white, but a new design would be cool. I know a guy who lives down the street whose moms name is Honey. Not sure if tats her real name. I don't have a steady girl right now but I really like this girl named Betsy from Southwest Philly. Shes my buddy's cousin. I saw reservoir dogs last year. Great movie but kind of twisted. I think you'll like it. On TV, I like Seinfeld or any sports that are on. I also like the Wonder Years and 90210. I've never seen Minder but it sounds like what the mob do around here. You have the mafia in Scotland? Talk to you later

Ferris

I had to read it about three times. I forgot half the stuff I'd said to him since it's been a few weeks since a sent the last letter. I wish you could see what you had written before so you'd have some idea as to what cunts were oan aboot.

My auld man is gawn mental at the news that MI5 is run by a bird. "Nae wonder this country is gawn doon the tubes" Her name is Stella Rimington, "Rimington? Sounds something ye'd pit roon the toilet befuck"

He saw it on cable that got installed the day, Telewest it's called. New phone number anaw, we were 3432487 for years, now it's 538 something.

I phone Harry wi the new number and he's oan aboot wanting tae get a pint. He's some man like. We agree to meet doon The Boom Boom at One-O and that will gie me time to phone Honey. I ring her number and thankfully she answers. We gab a bit aboot Celtic Park and talking in the hotel n that and it feels great, like she genuinely liked it and mair importantly, me. We agree she is gonnae come through here on Setterday and I am chuffed wi that. Details to be confirmed on Friday when she phones me. I get dressed and think aboot ma life, great girl in it noo, got tae sort maself oot, plus even though these hun bastards are trampling aw over us the now, last night showed the potential ae the club. We get our fucking act together and we will burn fucking Ibrox doon. Thing is wi these cunts though is, well, it's hard tae pit yer finger oan it. It's like, eh, that time I was in the Casino at the West End, Stakis I think it's called, you get the odd win n that but deep down you know the odds are stacked against you. Like the result has awready been decreed and you're fucked no matter what. That's whit life has felt like fir me fir maist ae it but ye jist huv tae keep fighting ae? In the hope that one day your day will come, or rather, theirs will.

I'm dressed and oot the hoose, it's a sunny day and I've still got 20 bar in ma tail which will be sound enough for a good peev. This is the best av felt in ages like and I wish aw days were like this.

I was so bouncy like a daft cunt that a didnae spot that I was being followed. I was too fucking heid in the clouds to even feel the first punch to the back of the neck. I lurched forward and fell right on ma coupon. As I turned ta see what was happening, that coupon was then booted square in the middle of it and I realised there were three of the cunts kicking fuck oot ae me. Even wi the blow tae the heid I could hear yin "You Fenian bastard, leave her the fuck alone, away to the fucking chapel and find a nun you bead rattling cunt"

The thing aboot a doing is, and I've had two before, once efter a night at Dalkeith Miners when this auld cunt thought as wis eyeing up his Mrs and once ootside The Norhet when I was mistaken for anither cunt, efter a while you actually cannie feel anything. It becomes monotonous and then inspiring. Yer shrinks on the telly will never admit that but there comes a point that you can only kick a cunt so much before they come back at ye.

I don't know who called the Ambulance but I do know the first I knew was waking up in The Western and no the bar unfortunately.

I became aware of a strange voice in ma heid. American, singing, what the fuck? It's Dion. The Wanderer and I realise that av got headphones on. I pull them off and my

Ma and Da are there looking surprised, There's a nurse and, fuck me, Harry is there anaw looking up fae 90 Minutes magazine.

"Are ye awright son? kin ye hear me?" My Ma says.

I think I am. I tell them I am.

"Thank God" she says clutching her rosary beads. Rosary Beads, bead rattler, I start tae mind the doing.

After everyone cuddles me or, in Harry's case, a firm handshake, I am told I've been in a coma for five weeks. They were scared I'd never wake up. They do all the tests and I'm sound. Another few days and I'll be oot. It's no aw good news though. Harry says the boys in The Gunner had a whip roond fir me and bought me a season ticket for Celtic.

Aye, cheers.

He leans in close to me, closer than he's ever been and says "Whae did this? They're gonnie fucking die, av spoke tae Doyle"

Doyle. One Punch Doyle. John Patrick Doyle. Jake Doyle to his friends. Harder than Cindy Crawford's boyfriend. Nice guy but, as the nickname suggests, could hit you and you'd feel like an Inter-City 125 had just banjoed you. Soild rebel. Always stewards the marches. Mad into the Happy Mondays. Gitting oot the pokey soon, jist no the now but.

I think on this and remember. I know who it was. Findlay.

Boardroom, Celtic v Kilmarnock, Celtic Park, March 1ˢᵗ, 1994.

"There's very few people out there Michael"

There was a slight sense of gloating in Tom Grant's voice.

"Tom, real Celtic supporters will turn up, this Celts for Change mob are just malcontents looking for a seat on the board"

"Michael, this has gone beyond that, we are skint, the fans hate us, the media hate us, where do we go from here? Cambusfuckinglang? You and I both know that it's all pie in the sky"

Jimmy Farrell walked in.

"Good evening gentleman"

Jimmy took his coat off and hung it up. He looked round and looked puzzled.

"Eh, has Susan not been in with the sausage rolls yet?"

12

I spent the next few weeks in the hoose getting better. Of course the brew had stopped my money. A line had gone in on my behalf but nae money had appeared yit. Like the auld man said "Never tell them you're ill". Also it said on the news there are now one million cunts on the NHS waiting list. Then there is Honey. She had left messages n that but hadn't come through tae see me or anything. A lot of cunts, that cunt Martin's younger brar for one, would go in the huff about that but I kin see why. She probably knows as well. I cannie say I wisnae warned though eh? I bet the cunt is feeling pretty good aboot it. First though, I need tae phone Honey. Naw fuck it, I'm going through. Mibbe.

Sweet Child O' Mine is on the radio. Always loved that song but there is an echo to it, it's the auld man. He's singing slowly to it. I've never heard him sing anywhere other than the fitba and New Year pairties. There's mair but. He's looking right it me when he's singing.

I'm a bit unnerved by this as it occurs tae me I don't think he's ever looked at me like this and a sortae want him tae stop but at the same time a dinnae, you know that wy? He gits up off the bench, pushing the table away, and it makes me think of when the my Ma bought it as Trendcentre that time and then I wis doon there tae see Kenny Dalglish that time and then I click into focus again and he's put his hand on my shoulder. He looms dead at me and says

"No cunt and a mean no cunt fucks wi ma laddie, they are gonnae wish they werenae born son"

He looks at me a bit mair, then goes to sit back doon, pulls the table back in and continues tae read the paper.

Oh, father of the four winds, fill my sails, across the sea of years.

That was probably the most eye contact we ever hud tae.

13

I am feeling better today. Despite the fact that I've no heard fae Honey again, I'm no in as much pain. Harry phoned me there, asked me to come roond fir him and I fancy it. Celtic and Hibs both qualified for the League Cup Semis last night. Celtic actually scored mair goals than I've ever seen them score in my life, 9-1 at Arbroath so mibbe that is the reason for me being in a good mood. The Huns are playing Aberdeen the night at Ibrox and we are both praying they get knocked oot. We will listen to it on the radio no doubt. Av still got £200 bar fae the collection the boys hud. They raised £350 but bought the season ticket for £150. I'm gled as my money fae being on the sick still husnae come through. Harry telt me tae come roon for 6 and he would make ma tea, so that's another couple of bob saved as I've been eating oot the chippy a loat to save ma Ma cooking. I'll need to leave aboot half five but as it takes me longer tae walk roond noo. It's only a ten minute walk but my hip hurts like fuck when I walk too fast.

When I get oot the front door it's nice. I've no been oot much, except fir the chippy and Celtic. Am no scared tae go oot, but I am wary. I wish I'd took that doing along D Mains or somewhere as am no along there much and wouldnae have tae see the spot I took it every day. Still. I make it oan tae Pennywell Road and am doon Kibby's Hill but it's a strain. Thankfully Harry's stair door is open. They pit new doors on the stair last year and the cunt never answers his buzzer so you hud tae kick the fucking thing in if the back door wasn't open. In my condition there was mair chance of Harry making Steak the night and no his specialty of

Cheesy Pasta, then there is of me kicking the door in. I dinnae mind the Cheesy Pasta right enough. Especially if there is Toast wi it. Harry has a barry grill that cooks the toast perfect so it's a delicacy we have savoured often. The cunt also got a SodaStream for his Christmas. Meant tae be a hing that makes yer ain juice. Fucking pointless if ye ask me gieing that he hus a Shoprite next door tae his stair and their juice is only 29p a bottle. That's for Coke anaw tae. I get up to his flat and, as usual, the neighbours radge dug is oot. They need tae pull it in before ye can go and tap Harry's door as it bites cunts. Fucking thing needs pit doon. I nervously stand there as the auld man of the neighbours huds the dug back as I tap Harry's door. As usual the cunt takes ages, deliberately am sure, but I hear him getting closer to the door which he opens, looks at me like I'm the Poll Tax collector and then walks away leaving the door ajar. I walk in and close it, noticing that his toilet door is open and it smells like someone has just had a bath. I bypass the living room and kitchen and head intae his room, a state as usual. He's flopped on the bed reading what looks like the latest issue of Vox. I sit doon oan his unit and he hits me with it "Fucking unreal earlier" What? "My auld man asks me to get a letter fae his jaiket fir him, I go tae where it is hinging and what's there?" I dinnae ken? "My hash and skins, plus a roach" Fir fucks sake, what did he say? "He was awright really, but he did say he knew you'd be smoking it tae" Christ almighty.

We ponder this for a while and Harry pits oan the radio. Radio Scotland. The Huns game will be on it and we are desperate for an Aberdeen win. They are droning on about The Huns so Harry pits it oaf and pits some sounds oan, a mix tape he has done with Happy Mondays, The Charlatans and Inspiral Carpets featuring heavily. Harry chirps up "See the draw for the semis is efter The Huns game?" Aye? "Aye? on Sportscene, live, 10.35 the programme starts" Cool. Hibs and Dundee Utd are the other teams that have qualified wi us, I hope the other yin is Aberdeen.

The game goes back on and true tae form The Huns have gone one up so we sortay tune out. He's making Cheesy Pasta at half time he says. "By the way, if yer wanting juice, I've got the Sodastream mixers, jist no the filters, ken tae make it fizzy?"

We chew the fat aboot hings and he asks about Honey "So you've no heard fae her since ye got that doing?" Naw. "That's ootay order man, she should huv at least phoned ye likes, fucking cow" As he says that it hurts me, and I want tae punch him in the face fir it, but I keep cool and jist nod like a daft cunt..

Half time comes and he's intae the kitchen to fire up the Cheesy Pasta. It disnae take long tae make and it fair fills ye up. The cunt's no making toast but, nae bread. We fill two massive plates of it and head tae his living room tae eat it. His auld man isnae in noo. I ask him what his auld man concluded about the customs and excise like find "No much, what kin he dae eh? I'm 20 fur fucks sake, I'm auld enough"

On Harry's wall is a big Gorilla. It's a charcoal effect done with they sort of things that are like chalk but no chalk. I hate the fucking thing. It's massive and done by some cunt in the jail. One day I'd like to throw it oot his fucking windae. We demolish our pasta and head back through for the second half, Harry crashing the ash as we stroll to the room. The second half has started and Aberdeen are pressing. "Here, you heard ae this new band fae America, Seattle I mean, Nirvana" Naw. "Fucking barry by the way" Music is changing. I'm a Ska child laced wi a bit of Hip Hop and Reggae but it's dying and this grunge shite is taking over. I dinnae get it. Smacks of a shower of NME wankers who missed the boat on Ska trying to invent their own wee fad. Ska is fucking magic but it's dangerous. Brings the gither black and white and my auld man always says "They ey want us at each others throats". That's probably true but I feel no animosity tae the black man, far from it. Bob Marley is a hero of mine, Peter Tosh as well. Then there's Madness and Ian Dury, they embraced the culture and evolved their music. The Specials tae. Was a boy called Drew who lived along the street fae me that got me intae The Specials. I saw him coming along one day and he had like a Trilby hat on and a Harrington jaiket, wi the tartan inside, Fred Perry polo on. He looked barry. He telt me tae come tae his Ma's and listen tae this song, Ghost Town, I was only aboot nine at the time and had never heard anything like it. I got my Ma tae buy me it at Vinyl Villains in Elm Row when she was in Leith the following Setterday. She moaned like fuck as she normally disnae go further than Woolies at the Kirkgate. Drew telt me tae get it there as it hud been oot for a while by then and Vinyl always kept a hud ae the quality stuff. I was at the fitba when she goat it, Celtic v Dundee, so a forgot aw aboot it until I got back in and saw it on ma bed. I'd got a record player for my 8th birthday so pit it oan six times in a row. Magic, very far fae bleak man. The thing aboot it is....

"YEESSSSS!!!!" GET IN THERE!!!" Harry jumps up. Aberdeen have equalised ya fucking beauty.

We both clench our fists and Harry does a dance similar to Bobby Robson efter David Platt hud scored fir England against Belgium at Italia 90.

We spraff for a bit as the game goes intae extra time. We sit pensively listening, praying Aberdeen score again. The inevitable happens though and that bastard Ian Ferguson scores a winner. Deflated we slump at different ends of Harry's bed.

"Ach well, still got the draw tae come"

Harry fires up his telly, it's an auld yin and needs tae warm up a bit. Viv Lumsden is on the news and then we switch to BBC for Sportscene. They show The Huns game and we curse throughout. We get to the draw and Joe Jordan is there for Celtic at a now deserted Ibrox. Scotland hero Big Joe, scored in three World Cups in a row. Speaking ae Scotland, I'll no be back as long as the cunts play at Ibrox. The draw gets made and it's Celtic v Rangers and Hibs v Dundee Utd in the semis, in that order. That wanker Dougie Donnelly pipes up "We will now do a draw to see where Celtic will play Rangers" eh? We came oot first ya cunt, it should be in Paradise? They do a coin toss. Walter Smith is there for The Huns and calls heads, typical Hun, it's tails. Ya fucking beauty. We will murder them in Para... whit the fuck. As Joe Jordan starts to talk about the joy of being at home, Donnelly pipes up "That was actually the toss to see who calls first Joe" I look at Harry and he looks at me, mooths open, before we can even speak they have tossed again, Joe has called tails and it's heads, it's to be at Ibrox. I can hear my auld man, half a mile away, kick oor telly in.

And like that, they are at home. The blows seem to come from everywhere these days, like that doing I got. It's fucking relentless and it feels like every time we take one step forward, they take two. Why? I just dinnae get it, no cunt can be that unlucky.

Harry gets over his astonishment and is pleased with the draw. I'm pleased that we will get 18,000 tickets for Ibrox and ponder a huge support for us there. My mind wanders to that when Harry's auld man, Big Harry bounds in and shouts at me "There he is, Pablo Escobar" I get the reference right away so hit back with-aye, eh, for the pain eh? and he replies with a beery smile:

"Wrong answer, we'll need tae toss a coin tae see who gits the next one ae"

Boardroom, Celtic Park, March 2ⁿᵈ, 1994.

David Smith stood up to address the custodians.

"The figures are in from last night, the actual crowd was 7458, and 2349 of them were Kilmarnock supporters. Paying customers, in terms of Celtic supporters, were 1273. We have told the press there were 10,000 there last night but we have a problem, gentlemen. These figures mean we cannot cover our interest payments this month. We don't have another home game until March 26ᵗʰ and the way the media are

battering us, there could be even less at that than last night. I know all of you in here have Celtic at heart but we need to be realistic here, another strategy is needed"

Silence round the room.

Smith looked at Michael Kelly

"Michael, do you have anything?"

Michael was about to speak when his secretary came in and said

"Sorry to bother you Mr Kelly, the Bank of Scotland are on the phone and they say it's important"

Michael Kelly looked resigned.

14

Funny thing is I meet Harry's faither again no long efter it and he asked me if a'd heard the news? I was expecting a slagging when he says "Aye, the BNP won their first seat yesterday. Tower Hamlets" I looked it up later in the library when ah wis taking ma auld man's books back and it's in London. The cunt who won it is called Derek Beackon. Won by seven votes. It's near Millwall's groond and a lot of cunts make assumptions straight away but I worked wi a Millwall boy on the building sites once and this one time when I was short he lent me a Score so I've nae problem wi Millwall boys.

I probably think aboot Honey less now than ever, it's been months since I got the doing and I've no heard a thing fae her since I got battered and I'm no expecting tae. I've also jist realised av no replied tae Ferris for ages either. I better dae that soon. In all honesty av been keeping a low profile. Been gitting these heidaches and av only jist started gitting ma sick money through and am needing tae pay a lot of that oot tae cunts av tapped. I'm £330 in debt and it's gonnae take me ages tae pay that back. Av got tae go tae the Doctors the day, git mair pain killers. Dr Agrawal. You've got tae watch him as he's an awfy cunt for sending ye straight tae the Western and there's nae way ah ever want tae see that place again. I walk up the long way to it, avoiding the spot ah got battered and when I get tae the crossing I see Martin, he disnae look happy. Smells like he hus a drink in him when he approaches me. "They cunts better no win on Sunday" He means Hibs. They are in the final of the League Cup on Sunday. No against us. We lost 1-0 at Ibrox, a fucking mistake by Galloway. So now Hibs are our only hope of stopping the bastards win another trophy. Well, no Martin's. "Two cups in two years would be too much to take" I can't see it like. The Huns won the treble last season and look a strong bet for another given the complete mess Celtic are in. Liam Brady resigned and Frank Connor took over much tae my auld man's delight. "A good Tim is Frank, he will sort those shower of cunts masquerading as Celtic players oot" The talk is Lou Macari will get the job. I've nae bother wi that. Done well at Swindon and West Ham and he's a former player. Brady was the first manager we ever hud who wisnae a Celtic player and although the fitba was great, we never won fuckall. "I'm sure The Huns will be strong like" Martin sounds like he's trying to convince himself. Hibs have a decent team the now, some of their players are pretty good actually. Still, the thing is, they cannie ever seem to beat Hearts. Ever. I think it was aboot four year ago the last time they did and Hearts have gone aboot 18 games undefeated against them. Still though, Martin is fearful "Na, The Huns will win, they almost won The European Cup last season fur fucks sake".

I had no idea he was that drunk.

We part ways and I get up the steps towards the Doctors. I think about that cup final on Sunday, it's at Celtic Park, which disgusts me, and I really hope Hibs win. It will be tough though. They have some decent players like Leighton, O'Neill and Jackson but some absolute duffers like Hunter, Tweed and Miller. Plus I read Jim McCluskey is the Ref. Bleak, man.

Just as I'm approaching the quacks, ah see a wee honey

approaching, no mine like, but a honey all the same. She's a year or so aulder than me but ye ken that way burds always seem that wee bit mair mature than ye? Her name is Jojo. She has a polish surname I cannie really announce and we spraff for a bit before I need tae go, thankful that a wee bit time in her company had reassured me, before I head intae the ddoactars that everything downstairs is in fine working order.

I sit doon in the tiny waiting room efter gieing the receptionist my name. That was nae John Buchan of a walk that's for sure. There's nae good magazines as usual, a two year old Cosmopolitan and some back issues of The People's Friend, so I just stare at my Gazelles until my name is called, which is aboot 20 minutes later. Am always amazed by this as when I'm in the cunts room, he gies me aboot two minutes and then hands me a prescription or line for the hospital. Yet other cunts seem to be in there aw day. Fir some reason I want tae batter fuck oot ae him. This is no like me but av been gitting these feelings a loat. Last week I wanted tae boot fuck oot the post man because he has had nae letters for me. Letter, fuck, I need tae get back tae ma man Ferris. The cunt gies me the usual two minutes and says av got tae go to the Infirmary for *neurological* tests. Whatever the fuck that means.

15

I'm gonnae head doon The Gunner for the cup final. Harry and his crew are leaving fae there for the game early doors and they asked me tae go. I actually fancied it but am pretty brassic on this sick pey and in all honesty am no sure a could handle a crowd of strangers, plus I might bump intae that Hun bastard. So The Boom Boom it is. I get dressed to the sounds of De La Soul. I get there aboot 1-0 and it's what I expected, a few skint Hibbies and a few praying Jambos. I fancy a Becks but the barman has already shouted "Lager?" at me and av nodded like a daft cunt. I take my place at the corner of the bar where the telly is. Maist of the cunts here are sound, a lot aulder than me like, but good crack. Plenty of them ask how my auld man is, nane of them ask me how I am. I'm nursing the pint. I've got 17 bar in my tail and will need to stretch it aw day for Harry and co coming back. I'll have another pint at kick off and that will dae me, hopefully, til full time. It's maistly Jambos aroond me but the biggest headcase here is a Hibby, Henry. He moves right in beside me, grabs my shoulders, and goes "Intae these Orange baaassstaarrrdss!!!!" Which makes a few folk jump, raise eyebrows and the like but makes me feel the best I huv in a long time.

The game starts and we are gawn radge throughout. Hibs are getting torn apart and we roar them on tae dae better, especially Henry "cammoaaannn the Cabbage, destroy these manky hun cuuunnttss" It looks like it is heading for 0-0 at half time when suddenly Keith Wright bursts through, we stop dead, watching, praying he rounds Maxwell and puts Hibs one up. Suddenly he's down and

Agent Orange McCluskey has booked him for diving. I look at Henry who looks like he's just had his baws chopped off "fucking dirty orange, masonic, cheating, loyalist scum fuckpig BAAASSTTTAARRRDSS!" I echo this, albeit less vocally, which is actually no bad as, when we see the replay, it shows Wright clearly dived.

Half time and 0-0, no one says much, we have me a Tim, Henry a Hibby and a squad of Jambos scared of Henry so the atmosphere is bleak, man. I head in fir a pish and notice both traps are full but the trough hus nae cunt standing at it. This gies me the opportunity to peel off and see that the funds are at over £14, which is no bad considering av still got half a pint left. I emerge fae the bogs and notice there's a full pint in front of the one I already huv. Henry says "I got ye one in, dinnae worry aboot gitting me one back" I will though. Thing is the barman hasn't put Henry's pint up and it's clear he's forgotten about it. Henry tipples and shouts over the bar "Here you ya cunt, ready cash customer at the end of bar!!!!"

Henry turns tae me and says "Did ah ever tell ye aboot that Wembley trip aboot 10 year ago?" Naw? "Fucks sake, av organised the bus doon right, so we've breezed doon there on the Thursday night efter the last bell in here. So we git doon tae the digs on the Friday morning and the cunt thit owns the digs takes one look at the bus fae ae us cunts and goes 'no way mate, no way facking way' so ah says tae the cunt 'listen pal, we'll flatten this fucking place quicker than the Ra, cause I can tell he kens am a rebel right, but he's no wearing it so av got 45 fucking headcases on this bus trawling roond London looking for digs and aw these cunts are shouting 'Take us tae the Blind Beggar' and shite like that. We ended up kipping on the bus, driver wisnae happy like, still, it wisnae as bad as the following time" Why? "Well that wis the year it got cancelled eh? and then played later. Well, ah'd taken aw the money eh and then on the Wednesday they cancelled it fir fear ae bother, which wis a fucking relief" Relief? "Aye, see ah'd taken aw the money fir the bus, digs, and tickets, except ah'd done the lot in in here eh so when it was cancelled eh I was just like 'Sorry Gadgie, we didnae get a refund' and then went through the lounge fir a bottle of beer"

The second half starts and The Huns are taking a firm grip again. The inevitable happens and that prick Durrant runs through and lobs Leighton. The Jambos quietly celebrate. Henry and I stand staring at the telly praying for an offside flag that's never going to come. Funny thing is, Hibs start tae come intae it efter that and big Donkey McPherson only pits the baw intae his ain net. We go berserk and embrace, knocking over a pint and the barman comes over, a Jambo, and tries to make a fuss but Henry jist shouts "Pit another one oan the bar and stoap mumping yer gums ya humpty hearts cunt"

McCoist is coming on. He's a lucky cunt but there's no doubt this final is here for the taking for Hibs, then the cunt scores a flukey overheid kick and you know that's it. The Jambos are more vociferous in their celebrations this time and Henry says nout. Not a good sign. The final whistle goes and Henry shakes my hand, walks oot, then steps back and throws his pint glass at the dartboard.

The bar goes back tae normal and I wonder if it's worth me steying here. Efter a bit The Gunner bus comes back and ah get word that Harry and co. have gone straight doon tae Leith. Dinnae blame them but the cunts should have jumped in first. Then the first Huns come in. Folk are awright wi them as they drink in here aw the time. Ah tell the cunts to celebrate noo cause we will hammer them next week. Am no sure even ah believe it.

The pub fills up with dejected Hibbies and then a Hun appears at the door. He's a known wanker and his presence disnae go doon well. He tries to tag on tae the other Huns but they are no huving it. He shouts "Fuck the Pope and Johnny Doyle" and one of the Hibbies, BaaBaa, picks up a pool baw off the table and throws it at him. It misses him by inches and he walks oot oblivious. At that point I decide tae go hame.

16

I'm watching a cartoon called "Basketball Jones" which I soon realise is actually a music video for a Cheech and Chong song. I'll need to mind and tell that cunt Harry as he will lap it up. Macari is in as manager but no taking the team the day. Although I'm feeling very nervous, am gawn tae Ibrox. It's weird but ah never used tae get nervous before these games, now ah feel nervous aboot jist leaving the hoose. Ah got vallies fae Agrawal and they do help a bit but a couple of nights ago some fucking drunk auld women tried tae get in tae oor front door. She wis jist a pished auld slapper but it scared the shite oot ae me.

Things like that are happening a lot to me these days, scared ae my ain shadow. It takes aw ma energy tae no act like a fanny oan the bus through tae the game and pretend am jist one o the boys. Nae cunt would understand this feeling. Or care. The tapes are blasting which does help. It's a boy fae doon ma way that pits them together, see him oan the James Connolly marches. I dinnae really come on this bus but it's the only one fae Edinburgh that will go tae Ibrox, gits the maist tickets. Ma season ticket got me one. So nae erse kissing fae me. I spraff away tae a boy fae Niddry. He's younger than me and disnae sound like yer typical Nidron either. The bus pulls intae Chapelhall and I wis hoping tae be in a round wi him but he's scarpered.

The usual boring time spent in the shitty pub they stop at. Atmosphere like a fucking funeral hame. Naewhere in Scotland is the balkanisation of the country mair evident than in the fucking central belt. Every cunt who comes fae

one ae these wee toons think the fucking world revolves
aroond it. Plus they aw are, moistly, divided intae Tim and
Hun toons so it goes wioot saying they aw hate each other.
Thankfully we dinnae stey long and we're aff tae Ibrox,
passing jubilant scum on the way tae the game. Am still no
maself but this is Celtic at Ibrox so yev got tae make the
effort. It's almost pitch black by the time the game starts
and we are doing no bad. Frank Connor is technically still
the manager but Macari is in the dug oot. Despite a
horrendous October, we are actually daeing no bad here
and everyone aroond me thinks so. It's a relief tae feel like
this for once here as it's been 18 months since we won here
and the semi-final defeat still lingers. Second half comes
and The Huns are pressing, the inevitable happens and
McCoist scores, with three stands aroond me erupting. The
worst part aboot it, especially when it's at the other end fae
ye, is that efter it hits the net, there's a moment when you
have the time to think that it may no huv actually
happened, then it hits ye, the noise, and ye look at them,
bouncing aroond ye, an air of triumphant inevitability
aboot them. Like they know they are going to score no
matter what ye throw at them. Am fucking sick of it. This,
efter me gieing it tight tae The Huns in The Gunner last
week as well tae. Thing is, for once, we dinnae fold and
equalise almost immediately. A free kick is floated in and
Maxwell makes a complete cunt ae it and the ball falls at
Collins feet. He seems tae take a fucking age tae put it in,
cunts aroond me aw bouncing in anticipation, but then
calmly toe pokes it intae the net and we aw go bananas. We
should huv scored a few times efter that but Macari is oot
the dugoot and ye kin tell he's urging players tae get deep
and take the draw. In all honesty it's no the worst result

here as these cunts huvnae even lost a game this season. They urnae even that good tae.

I look at their cunty wee scoreboard, far smaller than oor yin, and it says 90 minutes when we get a corner. Collins sprints over tae take it which hus Macari huving kittens and turning away in disgust. "This is it" a voice behind me says. As Collins whips it in, aw us at the front hear someone, probably Gough, shout: "Right, this is the keepers ball" except before he can get the "Ball" oot his mooth, it's past Maxwell, some cunt jumps and, fuck me, it's in the net. There is a pause. Aye, a definite intake of breath from aw of us before we realise that it's in and all over. After the melee, I realise that it's Brian O'Neil who got it, in aff his shoulder he said on the radio efter. Like I gie a fuck what it went in aff, as I once telt a burd.

17

Christmas. I used tae love it but am now dreading it. Av no been oot much and am constantly fucking brassic lint so av not got any cunt fuckall. Martin phoned me tae go oot, cunt ah nearly fainted when he did, but ah couldnae make it. Cunt is going oan a works night oot. Needs a word wi hiself. Work night oots are the last step before hinging yerself. I jist sit in ma room maist nights now, listening tae music or reading autobiographies that ma auld man picks up fae the library. Ah read The Moon's A Balloon by David Niven and For It's A Grand Old Team To Play For by Ronnie Simpson. Passes the time. Ma auld man broke his wrist last night. He told ma Ma he fell but telt me later that he's knocked a boy out efter gitting intae a fight aboot Yasser Arafat's first visit tae Britain. Said this Jambo cunt was saying that he wis a terrorist, ma auld man said "They said that aboot Mandela", the boy said something about the IRA and ma auld man knocked him out. Says he will need tae go tae the doctor but he's no taking any time off. I got another line fae the doctor last week, six months, and handed it in to Castle Terrace last week. Sick pey is shite, no as much as brew money but it least ye dinnae need tae sign oan fir it. I'm oan a book. Take it doon tae the post office every Monday. Nae worries aboot giros coming through the post now, the money just sits in the book waiting tae be collected each Monday. I used to get £68 a fortnight, now ah get £31 a week. Nae wonder am always brassic. That's why ah cannie afford presents anaw. Been six months now since ah got that doing, ye'd think cunts would undestand but am sure my Ma hates me noo and ma auld man, ah dinnae think, hus ever liked me. He did go oot looking fir the cunts that battered me, him and Dougie, roond aw the pubs and that but came up with nothing. It's like he fucking blames me fir that anaw.

Av no seen Harry much the now either. No since that night when he should huv been in The Gunner bit didnae appear efter the Hibs cup final. Fuck him anaw then, ah don't need any cunt.

18

Hogmanay. Fucking depressing. Celtic have completely fallen apart and a loat of cunts are now boycotting. The New Year game v The Huns is a must win fir us. Av no been invited anywhere for new year and that suits me fine. The Tories are gawn oan aboot "Back To Basics" well that suits me fine. Av only goat a tenner so a kin either buy ma boattle or go tae the game, so there's only one winner. A'd love tae take a boattle tae the game and smash one ae they Hun cunts over the heid wi it. Especially that one Hun cunt. The game is a fucking joke and am no wanting tae talk aboot it.

I go tae my Nana's but it's only my Grandad who is in and he takes an age to answer the door. He's raging as he's jist read in the paper that David Dimbleby is hosting his first Question Time efter Robin Day retired or died or some fucking thing. My Grandad says that David will never be as good as his faither, Richard.

Efter about 45 minutes there's still nae sign of my Nana so there's nae chance of a biscuit although my Grandfaither does offer tae make fried ingins but I decline. Plus it says in the paper under the Dimbleby story he forced on me that there is to be a "Lesbian Kiss" on Brookside the night and I wouldnae mind seeing that so I shoot back hame.

Upon returning my Ma tells me that The Joker fae Batman is deid.

19

Efter being battered oan the pitch by The Huns, 4-2, I
wonder if life is worth living. Ma mates huv deserted me,
ma team is fucking shite and ma burd hasnae been in touch
wi me in six fucking months. Maybe she's deid? I lie oan ma
bed and think aboot her funeral, would be a big posh do,
her auld man would see tae that, then ah think of the cunts
fae Reservoir Dogs being the pall bearers. Come tae think of
it, the cunts are already dressed fir it. Nice Guy Eddie could
dae the sermon. All the while Steven Wright talks over the
speakers in the Chapel. Chapel? Am no even sure if she's a
Catholic? Still, ah want tae hear him so we will go wi that.
Mind you, he's K-Billy, a Billy, no sure about that yin, a Billy
Boy maybe? Probably why the cunt sounds so depressed
aw the time. Never mind aboot the lights going oot in
Georgia, they are going oot on all these Hun cunts anaw. Mr
Blonde looks like a young Jock Stein, kin yese no see how
fucked ye are ya Hun bastards, how far the odds are against
ye noo? Then that polis boy would come in, like ye see at
weddings, but instead ae urging her no tae get married, he
wid be urging her no tae die and he would huv a Huns top
oan, and ye'd realise it wis that Hun cunt who is obsessed
wi her, the cunt that battered me wi the help o his mates,
paint by numbers, batter wi numbers, always the Hun way.
Except I'm the winner this time ya cunts, am in the front
row of the pineapple tae see her oaf, no you ya Hun cunt.
It's me thit Nice Guy Eddie is looking at when he talks
aboot lost loved ones, no you. Joe Cabot sits next tae me,
hus tae be a Tim wae a name like that eh? Reminds me o
Martin Meehan fae Sinn Fein so that will do fir me. Ah came
in the front car, the one right behind the one wi the coffin

in. You came in the boot, jist like that polis cunt. Yer aw the same, Huns, Polis, Dole cunts, Traffic wardens, aw think ye kin aw dae whit ye want. Well ye might have shot one ae us but this just in...ye shot Mr Orange ya fucking idiots, ha ha fucking ha! Whae's laughing now! Did the name no gie ye a clue that he wis one o your mob, naw? Ye'll no make it tae the front of the Chapel ya cunt, you'll run and gie it a go but that fit ye jist tripped over is fae Mr White. Mr White is going to stop you, MR WHITE IS GOING TO STOP YOU ALL!!!!!!!!!!!!!!!!!!!!!!!!!

My Ma shouts up asking what aw the commotion is. I tell her av got a video on and hope that she doesn't mind that av no got a video recorder in the room. I go doonstairs and my auld man tells me that Princess Michael of Kent has joined the Catholic Church. He sees that as a leveller for us after the recent defeat from The Huns.

It cheered him up an aw as oan the way hame he saw two cunts who were going to play Bowls and my auld man fucking hates Bowls. It's cause he read somewhere that Bowls was invented to keep the working class oot the boozers.

I watched a programme called *The Day Today* which has just started. Once I tipple it's a piss take, it could well be the funniest thing I've ever seen. The boy who does the sports reports is superb but ma auld man stands and looks at him for two minutes and says "Posh arsehole"

20

It's becoming apparent tae me that Celtic are in real
trouble. They are losing every week and every day in the
paper there is mair crisis talk. Scotsport Extra Time, which
I now see on the Friday night cause am nivir in the pub
now, is ey opening up with "And now the latest from the
crisis at Celtic Park, here is Gerry McNee" and then the cunt
will be like "Well Jim, it's more bad news for Celtic..." It gets
worse though. Ah heard ma auld man gawn bananas
doonstairs "FUCKING RAG! DON'T BUY THIS PAPER
AGAIN!!!" I go doon tae see what aw the fuss is aboot and in
front of me is the *Sunday Mail* and on the back page is the
headline "CELTIC R.I.P." and there's a cunt wi a top hat on
and black coat in front o one of they cars that coffins go in
which ma auld man reminds me is called a Hearse. I
immediately think aboot that mad night ah hud thinking of
Honey's funeral last month. Or kid on funeral. In fact am no
calling her Honey any mair, Heny will dae fae now on. Ah
stand looking at the paper and something snaps intae life.
Ah cannie put ma finger oan what it is but ah realise ah
dinnae feel scared any mair. I feel angry but not
argumentative or intolerant of cunts. Could be a passing
phase but I cannie mind the last time ah felt like this. I go
back upstairs but the mood follows me. I turn on ma stereo
that my ma goat me for Christmas and put in a tape, Ice
Cube, *Lethal Injection.* I pit side two oan and fast forward it.
Efter a bit of fucking aboot, a git it where I want it and
press play:

"You gonna walk with your enemy
before you learn to walk with one another?

How sick can you be?"

I listen intently. The words are swirling round my head, round and round and round.

"Where you gonna go when the brothers wanna bust a shot
where you gonna go when I wanna kill bloodclot
Supercat said that the ghetto red hot
bust a gloc, bust a gloc, devils get shot
nappy-headed, no-dreaded look where ya read it
buck the devil, buck the devil, look who said it
listen what I say after 1995 not one death will be alive
god will survive, him protect the civilized
who really cares if the enemy lives or dies?
not me, not me"

The cunt is right.

"you don't care if me die from the cracka
you don't care if me have a heart attacka
you don't care if me get car jacka
you don't care cause you're nothing but a cracka"

I've been a fucking idiot. A fucking moron. Fuck the *Sunday Mail* and The Huns, and all those cunts who think Celtic are deid. Also, fuck those cunts who battered me, your day is coming.

Awoken at last, I write to my pal and post the following at Drylaw Post Office.

Hiya pal

Sorry I've no been in touch recently. Basically I got battered about six months ago and have been recovering. Physically I'm alright now but mentally, well, they are no sure. The worse thing is that Honey hasnae been back in touch with me since. I really want to get back in touch with her but the guy who battered me, with his mates, is a this guy who is obsessed with her a bit and am no suire whit tae dae. To make things worse, he's a Hun(Rangers Fc fan) and they are ours(Celtic) biggest rivals. So what am asking you pal, and I know you're good with affairs of the heart, what would you do to win her back?

Your pal
Sidney

Come on Ferris, rescue me.

21

The Snooker is on when I get back in. Am no sure what tournament but auld man says "This is the boy ah wis telling ye aboot" Av nae clue whit he is oan aboot but pretend ah do. I look at the screen and see a guy aboot ma age screwing a baw back intently wi the rest.

The next shot is easier but he misses an easy one. I tell ma auld man that he disnae look aw that but ma auld man says "Remember the name, Higgins, and no like Alky Alex, this boy is one of us".

I feel good aboot maself. Glad ah posted that letter tae ma man Ferris, I'm sure he will ken whit tae dae regards Honey.

The nurse is coming up tae see me the day, so I bolt tae the room and go for a couple of hours kip first. As usual, it's a crap kip and spoiled by a major urge tae pish. Even though the toilet is next door tae ma room, I lag in the bottle of juice I had last night. It was Lilt and still had a wee drop in it so the pish really is indistinguishable. I fall back asleep and am awoken by the door opening and it it's the nurse. She does her usual box ticking and it seems to be going quickly which pleases me as am never comfy huving other cunts in ma room. Like usual, efter a long pish again, am needing, so I excuse myself and go to the toilet this time. As am standing there pishing ah notice that I can see through the slit in the carsey door and my ain room door. I can see the nurse and it hits me for the first time that she is quite tidy. Her neck looks appealing but I freeze as she turns roond, maybe she knows am watching her? Fuck. I don't think so though as she pauses like she is trying to hear, as ah can't hear anything over the sound of my own pish, av no idea what but ah keep looking at her and she moves really quickly. Aw fuck.

She's just had a swig of the Lilt bottle.

Ah breeze back in and she looks at me funny, she mumbles something about getting her skates on and asks if she can use the bathroom. I oblige but all I can hear are taps running.

Each tae their own.

I phone Harry. He seems surprised tae hear fae me and immediately invites me tae the Hibs v Celtic on March 19th. I don't hesitate and we agree to meet at Pearces at 9am that day. Feels like yisterday that we were in there efter the Race Night last year. Levski Sofia also fucked The Huns oot in the first round this year. I decide tae go doon tae Martin's hoose. I used tae go there aw the time but ah realise that av no been fir ages. I love his hoose like, he's got a new yin, well his Ma hus, at Salvy, in front ae the stables and it's a good yin, always something going on. I breeze through the shops at Muirhoose, and head oan tae Pennywell Gardens, through Pennywell Grove and look up and see that boy I know's hoose, him that does the tapes oan the bus, fellow Tim but total waster, nivir oot The Gunner and nivir missed a Celtic game either, fuck knows how he does it, wouldnae mind finding oot one day.

I'm over tae the main drag and there's fuckall traffic, over, and in the gate that leads intae the Brookside Close lookalike although av niver seen any Lesbians kissing here. His door is ey open but it's polite tae knock. His wee brother John answers and looks disappointed. Wee prick. He shouts for Martin who shouts for me to come upstairs and then sort ae does a double take when he sees it's me. "How you doing man?" he says, I tell him fine and fire in his room, sitting on the bottom bunk bed, but at the end closest to the door so I can see the computer screen that's on. He's got a barry new computer and is playing a manager game, asks if I want to help him? I agree and with him supporting Hearts and Arsenal and me being a Celtic and Liverpool man, we choose Nottingham Forest on account of our Stuart Pearce obsession. We have loved him for years and there are loads of reasons, his cool celebration after his free kick in the 1991 FA Cup Final, his tackle against Kevin Gallagher, hard as fuck but fair, in a game v Coventry and that animal bastard Basile Boli headbutting him in Euro 92 and Pearce brushing it off saying "The boy just bumped into me". Fucking wanker that Boli.

It's a good night, despite him putting on Nirvana, and I end up talking to him for ages which isnae like him. As I leave, I ask if I can borrow a couple of videos from him and he says nae bother. I choose The Man With Two Brains cause it's funny as fuck and Basic Instinct for the chugging potential. As I lift up Basic Instinct I clock the video underneath it, Ferris Buellar's Day Off and protruding from that is Reservoir Dogs. Honey.

Never mind "Save Ferris", Save ME Ferris.

22

Easter Road. Easter Road they play. I don't go to see them every other Saturday though. I go when Celtic go cause that's who I am. Thing is Hibs are on as much a downer as we are. They were playing well but then Hearts knocked them out the cup at Easter Road and made it 21 games undefeated against Hibs. After the usual session in Pearces and then The Elm Bar, we are walking along Montgomery Street pished. I'm looking forward to today. I read in the Scotsman that a young boy, Simon Donnelly, is in the squad today. Saw him at Ibrox in the Glasgow Cup Final, reserve game like, and he looked really good. Macari rates him, but apart from that I have high hopes. Hibs are a funny team, I know loads of cunts who support them and I like to see them do ok, hope that doesnae change. On the way we get cracking to a family of Hibbies from Campbelltown . Fuck knows where that is like but they seem nice enough. I ask the wee guy what he thinks the score will be and he says "2-0 tae Hibs". Wee prick. Reminds me of Oor Wullie. Harry and I go oor separate ways at Bothwell Street and arrange to meet after the game. I walk up to the Dunbar End and meet a guy fae the bus who confirms that Donnelly is in the squad which gies us something tae look forward tae at least. The game is a drab 0-0 draw lit up by a great performance from our keeper Muggleton and a substitute appearance by Donnelly that yields a turn and shot that that just flashes over the bar. Even though he missed, it gave me hope for the future, something that had been light in recent times. For some reason, it kept me inspired until full time. I was meeting Harry at 6pm in The Iona so ah hud the time and thought fuck it, I'll go roond and try tae git the cunt's autograph. One problem but. Av not got a pen. Plus I wouldnae mind a photo but if av no got a pen there's nae chance o me huving a fucking camera now is there? I make a beeline for the main entrance and see a couple of cunts from the bus who are always there and always getting autographs. They must have shrines to Celtic in their hooses. Thing is I cannie look at one cunt straight in the eye as I'd heard a story that one day one of the boys went tae his hoose and found him baw deep in his Step Mum. Aye, technically they are no related but fur fucks sake. It's no jist that but, it's the fact that this cunt never even mentions women normally.

I also spy a boy who is fae Aberdeen. I mind seeing him in the strippers up there, Bubbles or Krystals I'm sure it's called, ages wi me he is but he was up on the stage gieing it laldy wi one bird. His name was Sam but we called him "Sam The Bam" as he was pure radge at the strippers, no one of these shanus moranus cunts ye meet.

I make small talk with them about the game and some players start emerging. The few fans there go for guys like McStay and Collins but I bide my time and before long Donnelly comes oot. He gies the impression that no one will recognise and no one does really, except me. He's got headphones roond his neck and a barry Sony Walkman by the looks of it so I ask him what he's listening tae. He looks startled and looks at me as if to say "Are you talking to me?" but in a nice way. I nod like a daft cunt and he says "Eh, normally Stone Roses but this is a bootleg of a new band" I'll be honest, ah huvnae a clue what a bootleg is but ask who the band are he replies "Oasis" and ah huvnae a clue who they are either but make a mental note tae check them oot. We are at that awkward point where no one knows what to say so I break the ice and ask him if he minds me asking him a question? He says "Not at all" and so I go for it, I just ask him straight out, are we going to stop those bastards beating our nine in a row? he looks at me and at first I think he's going to knock me spark out but then he smiles and says "Maybe not this year, but we will" That does me but he has something else to say "You want these?" and I look at him in disbelief and mumble an aye. He hands me a pair of fitba boots, HIS fitba boots and goes on the team bus. I stand there like I'm glued to Albion Road and watch the bus pull away. I look down and see the boots, Adidas ones, but there is a writing on that says "SI D". I look and think Sid. Aye, Sid.

Something is happening in the universe.

Board Meeting, Celtic Park, March 3rd, 2pm.

"Gentleman, we are resigned to the fact that we can no longer keep this club"

Michael Kelly looked crestfallen as he spoke.

Chris White wiped a tear from his eye. He loved Celtic but had long suspected they, as directors, had the tiger by the tail.

"We are going to take Fergus McCann's offer"

With that, Michael walked out.

23

Having a trained ear for what is hitting the floor behind the letterbox, I hear from my bed that the envelope has no glass front so it could well be good. Even though it's May, it's chilly, but I bound downstairs in the Hanes boxers my aunty sent and confirm what I thought. It's a letter from Ferris.

Sid,

You mind if I call you Sid? Anyway, I know the type of situation you're in. The gang that I run with is called P.I.E (Posse in Effect) and we are always throwing down with the Junior West Mafia from Wynnefield Heights. They like coming down to South Philly to start trouble because they have more money than us, drive nicer cars than us and are friends with all the cops so they get away with everything. I thought this girl was cute that stayed around the way from me. Long story short, one night Junior West came down and attacked me and my two friends while she was watching and we were outnumbered 12 to 3. We got beat pretty bad til I picked up a steel jack and cracked one of them in the ribs. They scattered but it didn't look cool or tough. Anyway, I finally got the courage to talk to her a couple days later and she thought I did what I had to do. She said at some point you have to do what you have to do to protect yourself and your turf when you're outmanned, outnumbered and out-resourced. And at the end of the day, you gotta stay true to your values. I think she's right. So what would I do if I were you? Talk to Honey about what happened without explaining anything and see what she tells you. That'll let you know everything you need to know. Take care of yourself bro, I enclose 10 dollars to go on a date. Boat trips are always good for a date.

Ferris

I study this a lot and think that it's daft but maybe no. I check the hiries and see ah huv jist enough tae get the train through tae Glesgae, then the bus tae her bit and then aboot a fiver left efter that cause of the 10 dollars which is aboot half bat here. I'll go fir it. First though, business. He's been spotted see, Charlotte Square. My auld man's buddy Dougie put his peelers on him for three days in a row and buzzed me on the quiet. See Dougie was the only cunt ah could really talk tae aboot the doing and he built up a picture in his mind o the cunt, like they American detectives dae n that. Oh and he also knew his registration number and clocked it pulling in to they parking spots roond that park in Charlotte Square that only posh cunts git tae use. Dougie is wider than trap six and spotted that the cunt was using the first office on the second part of Charlotte Square every day so set the trap. I was going to sit on his car bonnet and bounce til the alarm went off. When the bastard came rushing oot, Dougie and my auld man were going to leap oot and fucking banjo the hun cunt. As plans go, it was up there with fucking Normandy Beach.

Like the dust that lifts high in June, when moving through Kashmir.

The morning of the action, Dougie phoned me and telt me

he had turned up as usual. I ran up and jumped on a bus tae the west end which took ages but I wis still early. I walked doon and saw the van first, the two of them, my auld man and Dougie, sat there like The Sweeney on a stakeoot. Just beyond the van was the car, his car. Fucking Findlay. This was payback. I even put my Hoops on for added spice. I walked past the van and nodded like a daft cunt at them before sitting on the car. I felt no apprehension at this at all, it's written in the stars, SI D. Sid. Send In Dougie.

I sit on the car and start to bounce but there's no much give in it at aw. It's an expensive cowie like so that's expected. I'm thinking aboot this a bit when a guy stops and smiles at me. It's no Findlay. I focus in and I don't recognise him at all. He moves forward and says "You ok there friend?" I tell him I'm fine and he nods towards the Hoops and says "Bhoys are on their way back I think" I agree and see now why he stopped. He's mid-30s, rucksack on the back and a pleasant manner about him. I feel comfortable enough to tell him oor plan and he smiles and says "Violence isn't the answer my friend, our revenge will be the laughter of our children" and he walks away. Told me his name was Jim McGuigan.

I think about this and go to the van, the alarm still hasn't gone off and I put the case that maybe it's no the best way to respond to violence with more violence and Dougie looks like I've just shat in his tea but my auld man beams "That's a man talking there son"

I tell them I've got some stuff tae dae and make my way to Haymarket station. I could have sworn that was closer to

Charlotte Square but it doesn't feel like it. I get my tickets and breeze doon, occasionally I chance no buying them and hoping for nae guard but nae risks there today, jist gawn through here today is a fucking risk. The journey normally crawls in but in typical fashion it feels like I'm on it then off it and already heading for the bus stop to get to Honeys. A thought crosses my mind, what if she's moved? Ah fuck it, I get on the bus anyway and it's a nice day plus ah need time tae think so I jump aff a stop early. I'm walking up thinking of what Ferris said and I look at his letter again. His PS says he would be happy to wire me money but in all honesty I've nae clue whit that means.

I approach the door and knock it. I'm expecting her faither

tae answer knowing my luck.

She opens the door.

Does a double take when she sees me.

"Hello Henrika" is what I say to her, the first time I've ever

used her full name.

She replies "Hello" in a way that makes me think she's

forgotten my name.

For some reason, I think of this guy Tony, he's Martin's

faither but I barely see him.. Anyway I'd went doon for

Martin this one time but he wisnae in but Tony said "come in"

Gave me a can of Export.

Wee John was there.

Efter the cans finished Tony said we should aw fire doon the Commodore Hotel.

Wee John said it was gitting done up, impressive knowledge for an eight year old,.

So we went along The Lauriston Farm and Tony got the scoops up. Wee John got a coke.

Waitress says, just casual like, "You lot not going in for the quiz?"

She had a badge on saying Nicola and wisnae a bad bit o gear.

She wis aboot tae get some o the Dempsey charm when Tony goes

"How? ye trying tae say we're aw fucking thick like ya cunt"

She stood in the doorway when I was thinking about this and she was aboot tae talk when I put my finger over her lips. She looked a wee bit scared but then smiled and got intae it. I telt her no tae say a word, it was fine and said that we should go on the boat tae Rothesay, huv a wee day of it. She nodded but didnae look a daft cunt and went in tae pit a jaiket oan and "freshen up". At this point I felt guid, then as I turned he was right there, I spied the car first, personalised licence plate that should read I AM A CUNT, like aw ones should. He stood there in front of me and scowled "You fucking shit, you think you can sit on MY car and get away with it? You think you can set ME up and I'll just take it? ME? ME? You scumbags must know YOUR place. It's beneath US. THE people. WE ARE THE PEOPLE!!!!!!!!!!!!!!"

At that point I took a step back and his smile got wider, in his ritual humiliation of me. He saw me back away and took this in a triumphant manner, as was his wont. His was smiling and enjoying himself so much that he didnae see me take the scaffolding hammer, that Dougie gave me, oot ma back tail, so he had no chance of seeing it when I took it right across his fucking coupon. He went down instantly, out cold but no deid, just enough to know the score. You may be the people, but this is our world and we're taking it back.

Honey comes out and surveys the scene, she knows what has happened, not a daft cunt see, and again I motion to her to say nothing. She steps over Findlay and takes my hand, we walk to the bus stop, which has the bus that fires down to Rothesay. It's a lovely day and when the bus comes it's an easy choice to make, we are sitting at the front of the bus now.

24

It's only when we arrive for the ferry do I realise that I've never been down here before. We are at Wemyss Bay for the boat over. I pay it and I realise I'm skint. FUCK. What the f...hang on, I've got that fiver from the money Ferris sent. Ya fucking dancer! I pull it out and like that, it's gone, right into the water. Honey is in the toilet so there is fuckall else for it, I have to dive in and get it. No one is looking and I'm a strong swimmer so I go for it. The water is dark and murky but I'm on a mission here. My eyes are wide open and as I turn left I see it on top of the water, it's appeared ten feet from me and it sinks due to being so it wet and I watch it float down effortlessly. It's pathetic that it's come to this, having to go through all this shit just to get money that a guy in North America has sent over but I'm leaping forward in the water and I've got it. Hallelujah. I swim to the shore and a guy with dark hair reaches out his arm and helps me onto dry land. I thank him and in my soaking state ask him his name as he leaves and he says "Matt". Just beyond him Honey looks at the scene, she comes over and asks if I'm ok and I reply that I am. I tell her I'm a bit wet but will Gloria Gaynor, she replies "So am I now".

25

We get across the other side on a boat called "The Saturn" and head for a pub in a hotel called The Victoria. She gets the drinks in and I'm about to speak when she speaks "Ok, it's my turn now, be quiet Sidney. I want to tell you something. You need to know why I wasn't in touch with you this long, you deserve to know. Well, after what happened to you, and I know what happened to you, I was ill, mortified, vengeful, humiliated, all those things. I bet you hated me. I bet you hated me, feeling alone and scared, all because of me and my ties to that complete moron Findlay. The stupid fool came to my house after it and told me expecting me to, I don't know, fall in his arms or something, I went scatty and threw him out and my Dad told him he'd call the police if he ever came back and he never did. Still, you didn't know this and so Sidney you must know this, so you can be at peace with it, the thing is I went to phone you and it was only then that I realised...YOU NEVER GAVE ME YOUR NEW NUMBER!!!!!"

Ah fur fucks sake.

Stairs of Celtic Park, Main Reception, March 4th, 9pm

"Good night Mr Smith, Mr Kelly"

David Smith and Michael Kelly looked up to see Fergus McCann at the top of the stairs.

"Goodbye Fergus"

They said in unison.

26

Amsterdam, Present Day.

I'm glad av got a book wi me. People-watching is barry, especially in Amsterdam's cafe culture, that's cafe culture by the way, no cafe society like in Paris or what that cunt Cameron is trying to create in London. £26,000 a year is the limit of Housing Benefit you can get in London now, Daily Mail readers are aghast right up until they realise that their drum cost £3m and it's only as close to the west end as Tilbury, but you do git bored wi people-watching efter a while. The reason is most of us are the same. The disnae fit well wi divisive politicians and arms dealers but it's fucking true and the only time you see someone's real character is when they are backed into a corner. That's when you find out about a cunt, whether you can rely on them or whether they'd sell you oot. That's ma theory anyway. Take it if ye want. The story I'm reading is by an auld pal as well. It's called "Sound track of the New York Waterfall" I slide down my Marley headphones and pick it up:

"We can hold our heads high today", Tommy was in a statesman-like mood. "No hiding under the fucking dashboard this time my friend, you got it", Yeah, Ok Tommy, I get it. It was a rare treat this for me. After months of pleading and cajoling I'd finally convinced Tommy to take his new car out and get us the fuck out of Jersey and down to fucking Florida for some serious sun, sea and sugar doobie doop doop do do.

"Did you talk to Chas?" Chas was our man in The Bronx, you

want something in The Bronx, talk to Chas. The Bronx motto is "Only the strongest survive", amen to that.

I talked to Chas. "Good, I like to let him know what's going on" There are many stories about Chas but my favourite is about him and his right hand man Kevin Devine. They had this thing going where people came to them if they had problems. The cops didn't like it, they had to be the law round there and so shut their streets down. The whole area expected a backlash but nothing happened, people started to question Chas and Kev, had they lost their grip? Then one summer morning, as the sun came up, people started noticing it, you couldn't miss it really. See Chas and Kev kept cool, did their homework and found that their part of The Bronx was old Indian land and what do you know but didn't they find some native American blood in their crew as well. So the sign was very apt YOU ARE NOW ENTERING FREE WOODLAWN. What better a "Fuck you" to the cops. They'd call when we hit fucking Florida. Free drinks in their bar too, for those who can afford it that is.

He's a worrier at times is our Tommy, a non committal type for long term stuff so getting him to do this, to drive to fucking Florida, is an achievement I should list on my C.V. Sometimes you ask him something and the second you say it you wish you hasn't bothered as you know it's going to worry him. He loves his wife see, but he worries about what she says, man and wife shit that everybody gets but he doesn't roll with it. One time we were going to Yankees-Mets at the old Stadium, the time when it was $7.50 a beer, and it gets rained off, so I'm like great, lets hit a bar, only $5 a pint too, but right away panic has set in on Tommy as he tries to work out how long it will be before his wife tipples that the game *has been cancelled ergo how long he has in the pub. So you get used to the look of dread in his face any time you mention pleasure. They say Sammy The Bull was home at 6pm every night so I guess there is precedent.*

Funny thing was that night in the bar, I saw this guy I thought I had recognized. I waited and listened, he had the black Mets top but the accent didn't go, it had to be, Harper? he spun round and looked at me "Jesus Christ, how's it going?" What the fuck you doing here? "I got a cheap flight and wanted to make a weekend Subway Series, Christ, what a fucking start eh?" We had tweeted back and forth a lot but still, this was some coincidence. David Harper, diehard Celtic and Mets, half a good guy as they say in New York. Teehee.

I was never in cars much as a kid, most people couldn't afford them although all my aunts and uncles had them, the only places I ever traveled were to the football and we always went by supporters bus. There were three occasions I recall that we went by car, all in my Uncle Francey's. The first was in 1980, to see Celtic play Hibs in a Scottish Cup semi-final. I got to see George Best play, albeit for Hibs, but more importantly I got to see Bobby Lennox play and score for Celtic. At 6 years old I didn't realise the significance of it but I do now and to have seen a Lisbon Lion, and absolute gentleman to boot, play in a competitive game still gives me a warm glow. The second occasion came shortly after that when Celtic played Rangers in the Scottish Cup final. Everything seemed to be going the same way as the semi, Mark Henderson and I were crammed into the back of a hatchback, My Uncle drove, My auld man drank, Mark's Grandpa Archie regaled us with his stories and Jake Wilkie looked menacing. As we were on the M8 just coming into Glasgow, a Rangers supporters bus pulled up beside us and were giving it laldy towards us. Mark and I, as kids, were giving it back, when Jake opened the door, calmly walked over to the bus, pulled an axe from his coat and started to attack the bus much to the bewilderment of the passengers and bemusement of our car. They pulled away at first opportunity. Of course, this was just a warm up to what was about to occur. After 1-0 extra-time win for Celtic, where my hero Danny McGrain hit a shot that George McCluskey deflected past The Girvan Shitehouse, the huns invaded the park which prompted a huge surge from the Celtic end to get them. I'd love to say I was on the park chasing the bastards all over Hampden but I was six, I remember the heat, the goal and the dust. The Celtic end didn't even have concrete on it at this point and when we scored, dust was everywhere. We had moved to the back to get the kids(Mark and I) out safely(I love that concept by the way, adults drinking all day, attacking huns with axes, bringing them in to mass throngs of drunk people but as long as we get ready a minute from the end we will be fine!). Danny went up to get the cup and we were away before the proper riot happened. Well, most of us were, one stayed, if you need to ask who, you need get out more.

2-*"I never lie because I don't fear anyone. You only lie when you're afraid."*

"What about that fucking bar last week? You're in the car all this time and no mention? what the hell is wrong with you?" Tommy is still fuming at this bar we went in last week, a rooftop bar in Manhattan, fucking $6 a bottle as well. We had a reserved table courtesy of the best looking girl in Manhattan, and about two minutes after we had taken our seats, a waitress comes up to us and asks us to move as the table was reserved. Knowing the consequences of her actions, I immediately replied "Yeah, it's for us baby" and she quickly apologized profusely. I didn't want to look at Tommy because I knew what look I'd get, so I looked at the big TV and said "Oh The Belmont Stakes soon?" and slowly made eye contact with a his fearsome expression "Don't embarrass me". What? "I am going to throw her cute little ass off this fucking roof" They gave us free drinks and at least three managers came over to apologize and I managed to get him out of there quicker than the IMF guy out of his hotel room but it was no good, he was seething and a week on, hadn't simmered at all.

He forgot about for a bit because when we went to Muldoons, a more sensible $4.50, Michael Tomisser was in and he was even more pissed than Tommy. Grabbing me straight he said "Boy am I glad I saw you, did you hear this shit about the Red Sox buying Liverpool?" He was a die hard Red but die hard Red Sox hater. "It can't happen, this is like losing your girl and then she says she will come back but only if she can fuck Ted Malone as well" Ted Malone? "Yeah, you know, Sam from Cheers" Relax Michael, let's a have drink. Michael is a really good looking guy, he should have no worries. 12 shots later, he didn't "Walk on, wwwwwaaaaaalllllllkkk oonnnnnn" and then he collapsed.

"All week I've been thinking of what I should about it" Tommy is not a guy to cross but if you're ever in trouble, there is no one on the face of the earth you'd want your side before him. No one. This one time I got a ticket for a Subway Series game from Stubhub, I had other sources but just wanted no fuss, go, no problem. It was a Sunday afternoon game and on Saturday night I realized I hadn't printed the ticket off and had no paper. I had mentioned it to Tommy in a text and got no reply, something that happens a lot as he always losing his phone or sometimes he just assumes you know what his answer will be so he doesn't reply. His words, not mine. So I forget about it and am watching TV when a reply comes in from him "Come out". What the fuck is he talking about? Then my bell goes, I go to the door and there he is with a package of paper. That's Tommy, guys like him are a dying breed and they broke the mould when they made this guy. And we won 9-3 Harper.

"I could blow the place up but there's a deli I like across the street, don't want them to lose any stock"

The thing is, there was already a backdrop to this trip and I suppose I should say that although Tommy sometimes needs pushed to have fun, every so often he just dives in head first. So on Saturday there, he put on his swimming trunks. So, what happened was I walk into one of the bars, a ridiculous $7, one night and see a look on the barmaid's face like "I need to talk to you immediately" Ok. I approached her thinking "this could be fucking anything here, what I have done now?" and the she hits me with "Have you spoken to Tommy since last night?" "Uh, no" I lied. Thank fuck, it's something he's done. "Well, he came in here last night all fucked up and saying inappropriate things" That sounds like every night, "and then he was doing shots, shouting and all that" At this point I was struggling to figure out what exactly the problem was? "Then when I finished I left and what happened was he left right behind me so everyone in the bar thought we'd gone together" Ok first of all, yeah and so what. Of course I knew they hadn't left together, so what was her problem? Months later I found out, she was fucking the barman on the side, he was also there and was pissed but couldn't like shout it out, so called her, asked her what was going on and she had to come back from her place in The Bronx just to prove she wasn't with him. Meanwhile, all the while, Tommy had just gone to another bar. "Ok, I'll talk to him, don't worry about it" Of course, I didn't, I made it look like I did but really I was just like "So why didn't you fuck her then?" joking and Tommy, being Tommy, was like "Who are we talking about here?"

3-"I think the brand mark would be sincerity"

I check the Yankee score on my phone and see they are 4-1 down at in the bottom of the 8th, like clockwork, a Tweet comes in from Jim McGuigan, "hahahaha Boston are moving into first place". Fucking Red Sox fans eh? Forever in the Yankee shadow, they can't enjoy anything without bring the Yankees into it. Even Mets aren't that bad, well I suppose they don't get much success but although Jason Higgins, my buddy, seems to think they are the best ball team ever. I was batting back and forth with him over the recent Subway Series and he was full himself the Friday night then disappeared the Saturday and Sunday, you can guess how the series went from there. The jealousy of the Yankees spreads far and wide, one minute I'm told they are the establishment team, the next that they are all savages who will murder you the minute you set foot in The Bronx. I do love going to Yankee games though, you can feel the history the minute you set foot on 161st St. The greats that went down there, Babe Ruth, Mickey Mantle, The Yankee Clipper himself Joe Di Maggio and modern day you can still see some legends like A-Rod and Derek Jeter and one God. Mariano Rivera is one of the few athletes in American sports there is no debate about. It's very hard to get No1's in American sports, the best NFL player ever? Tough, Basketball? Yeah Jordan maybe but real NBA fans know that Magic always had to go through Larry to win and vice-versa, Jordan never had that, not really. However they never argued against fact is that Mariano Rivera is the best ever closer in the Baseball. Nobody even debates that.

"Don't worry by the way, I'm packing" Tommy pats his

pocket. The kind of thing unnerves me with a cunt like Tommy; he literally could be talking about anything. You can't predict the thinking people like him, although they always think you can.

One time he was driving me to the airport, as we are going he starts talking non-stop, telling me that this would be the way we would go if we were going to Kearny from his house. All the time I'm thinking why the fuck would we be going this way to JFK? I think that out loud and Tommy says "We're not going to Newark?" before U-Turning the car in a way that would have Zoe Bell fucking shit her pants. I'd mention it now but he wouldn't remember, he never does. What about that Irish bar in JFK by the way? $9 a fucking Guinness!

"Hey, Went for a Hennesay family weekend during it I had to golf with Paul Hennesay, Jimmy and Michael and you know I hate golf, right? At the ninth hole, you know the turn? So I go for a piss and the bathroom is full so I go out back behind the Dumpster and there are two guys who work there and they are smoking pot. They freeze when seeing me and shit their pants. I give them the look of "You're fucked" grab the joint, take a toke or 2, piss and then go back to the best golf game of my life shooting a 127" Tommy could take advantage of anything and anyone. "Listen, let me ask you something that's been bothering me for a while" I didn't like the tone of this, I always get paranoid when people say things like this to me or when they ask to speak to me in private, it's normally pre-engaged on account of their complete inability to make any positive impact on the world so they set about taking others down, you never know what shit they are going to say and with a cunt like me, it could be anything.

*"How come no one ever makes of fun Dick Van Dyke's name?"
What? "It's got Dick and Dyke in it. What, you're gonna tell
me you never pondered that?" Pondering is not something I
do very often these days, no time, everything goes so fucking
fast here and it can drive you nuts, then you get used to it,
then it can drive you nuts again. Lots of things can drive you
nuts here, not least the fact that to do anything here you
both need nuts and the ability to drive. Tommy can do my
driving. "Something I have been pondering recently is going
buck wild with Betty White and Barbara Walters" Tommy
just looked at me as if I was crazy, not at the suggestion, I
think he was furious that Dick Van Dyke wasn't on my mind.
Constantly.*

*I enquire as to what the fuck he is packing exactly and it's
the entire Pink Floyd catalogue. Now I like Floyd as much as
the next dude, although I'm sceptical about some of their
stuff, but what this does mean is that Tommy is going to go
through lots of reminiscing about where he was when he
could first tell a green field from a cold steel rail.*

4-"I'm a man's man, I'm here to take my medicine"

Before the trip could begin though, there was a party, a small one, but still a "Bon Voyage" feel to it. In all honesty I was not in the mood for it at all, in Donovans in Woodside, $4.50, but I got to say now, it was pretty fucking good. It would have probably just ran the normal course of the usual parties in there, get drunk and risk your life with Tommy driving you home, but as we walked in and heard the voice, we both knew were in for a treat. Kenny, not that you'd know by looking at him, is a US Marine. He is one guy you want with you if anything kicks off because everyone underestimates him. He's not that tall, bit of a beer belly and very courteous to everyone. They think. He's a fantastic controller of places and can passively aggressively let everyone in the room know within five seconds he's in charge. When we go in he's already holding court....

"First time I ever heard the name of this place, I was an Altar boy, we're doing a wedding and the Priest leans over and says to me 'Kenneth, go down to Donovans and get the groom out of there"

We laugh and take our seats at the bar. He's got a young guy with him, we find out soon he's a fresh face from West Point but he's already done three tours of Afghanistan. This kid barely looks college age. "Hey, there they are, the world travelers, what'll it be guys? Kevin, set em up" We settle down and scoop up, it's been a while since we have seen Kenny but he heard we were planning a trip, got a few of the guys together and here we are. Kenny of course, was a mile a minute when talking and you barely get a chance to think never mind laugh.

"Hey did you hear about my brother? Yeah, he died, suddenly"

What the fuck?

"Everything was fine, he goes for a routine check-up, next thing it's an episode of House"

And we were off.

"I'm not saying my father is tight but he spends the night opening and closing the fridge door just to make sure the light has gone off"

I lean in to talk to him but it was no good.

"Hold on, call the guy from the Kings Speech, I can't understand a single thing Rod Stewart here is saying"

The rest of the night was spent drinking and listening to Kenny's war stories, literally. Almost. Frankie Fraser was in too. I like Frank, he reminds me of Dom from Entourage, kind of no nonsense New Yorker that epitomizes areas like Woodside. He was telling us about the second rise of the New York Cosmos when Kenny grabbed me again, "Yeah I forgot something, I knew I had a story for you, by the way when we gonna go see Celtic?" Anytime Kenny, "Good, so listen, it's about 1975 I think and my buddy grabs me, I say buddy, he's a good five years older than me which is huge at that age, and he says get your shit together, we are going to Yankee

Stadium. I'm in bits, seven years old and I am going to see the great New York Yankees, I almost pissed myself. So we jump in a car, I forget who's it was, and off we go. We get to the stadium and, you know, I'm all excited, and I'm looking round and there's only like 15,000 people there, at a time when the Yankees were on the rise and selling out all the time, right? So I turn round and before I could say anything, there he is right in front of me, the great Pele, and I realise, Jesus Christ this is a Cosmos game, I'll never forget it, Pele did a pass right in front of me that set up a goal, was beautiful. I stood there the rest of the game in awe. After the game I said to my older buddies that was great but I honestly thought we were going to see the Yankees? One guy turned round to me and says 'You think we'd waste a fucking Yankee ticket on you?' "

5-"I'm happy. I'm financially ruined, but what you gonna do?"

We drive off at speed from his house in Ringwood and, not being a yank, I've no real clue what road we are on or where we are about pass. Fuck you I know how to find North Korea on a map though. I think about Donovans again, what a fucking scenario last night. After Kenny left I looked along the bar and saw a woman to die for. Blonde not dirty blonde but could be one, body, hourglass, age, I'd say 37, look, naughty. I'm liquored up enough to make a move, I'd had more than one, and she looked over enough to be interested. So I slink over, apologising for the racket Kenny was making, "oh don't worry about it" straight away I clocked the accent wasn't Woodside. Forest Hills maybe? Na, there ain't any women over there with this amount of class. So I ask and..."I'm Irish Australian". She must live in Jackson Heights. At this point Tommy shouted over "You want another drink Burton? How about Elizabeth?" Some fucking wing-man him eh? We talked some more and I was down with her politics, she was a rebel heart no doubt, and I'm thinking play it cool, this is great and then we discuss personal lives and marriages etc, and at the point where I think she's clearing the decks to get something in between us, and the alcoholic haze is hitting me, the music is Sean South of Garryowen, she says it. I hear it but it doesn't register so I ask her to repeat it, and it's what I thought, the same surname as me. We talk more and it's your worst nightmare, related, and this is New York, not Alabama. We exchange Facebook details and hug, at this point a young guy comes in, James, it's her son, which is where it got too spooky and I leave her with "Another life Mychell". Hey, even Frank Sinatra didn't hit the all the notes on some nights.

*It's at times like this I ponder who I am, why I am here and where I came from. Who I am? Nobody. Why I am here? No idea. Where I came from? The Gunner. The Gunner was my local pub back in the day, £1.25 a pint then. It's a not bar in the American sense more a social club for the people that asylums reject. I did all my early drinking there and, although I did not know it then, it gave me the grounding that enabled me to come to America. For a start, The Gunner taught me to "watch points". This is the skill of being able to know what is going on in every part of the place you happen to be, bar, restaurant, whatever. See in The Gunner you had to because at any given time a fight could erupt. One true story from back then is when I was in The Gunner(lounge) and was sitting with a friend debating how bad our football team was. A guy he knew and I knew of came in and said he was in to "stab that cunt ******" After 10 minutes my mate calmed him down, got his knife and he had a drink with us and that was it. He went to the bathroom, said "Alright boys, cheers for that, gies the knife back and I'll go", my mate did and the guy promptly walked to the bar and slashed the guy right across the throat. Right across the throat but not the right guy. Mistaken identity. The guy lived, the other guy was never caught. Another one, I was maybe 19 years old when I went in and it was a Sunday night, karaoke night, which meant one thing, women. I had my eye on a few that sung and so didn't see this character approach me and only heard the second time when he demanded I buy him a drink. Shitting it, I went up and saw Woody, a great friend, older guy and complete lunatic. He asked who I was buying it for(watching points) and said he would take it over to him,* *he took the bottle of becks, calmly walked over, smashed it over the guy's face and calmly walked back and said, I swear, "When are the fitba fixtures oot by the way?". When you grow up surrounded by that kind of thing, you become hard, streetwise and wide as fuck. Also it's where my friendship with one of my real best friends developed. Hosey is very similar to me on lots of things and completely different on others. However when it matters, he's there. One time my team had a truly awful defeat and I phoned him to meet him in The Gunner but he told me not to come as everyone was waiting. Not only that, he took on all the mockers that night and he doesn't even support the same fucking team as me! I think the difference between my friendship with Hosey and everyone else is it's not that we share all the same loves, it's that we share all the same hates and someone who knows who to hate is ok in my book. We also marched together for what we believed in, when we were young and shouldn't have had a clue about anything, when our pals were out in white shirts and bad aftershave, we were marching for Edinburgh's Finest Son, James Connolly and when now, in 2011, a common phrase has came to the fore "We're not sitting at the back of the bus anymore", we were never prepared to sit at the back of the bus, which doesn't win you a lot of friends in Scotland but it certainly got me real one. As argumentative a cunt as he is as well.*

6-"Let me go through this RICO thing again. It says if anyone anywhere is caught doin' anything wrong, then everyone is guilty up and down the line. Wait a minute. This is a law?"

You kind of drive by a much of muchness once you get on the highway, McDonald's, Cracker Barrel, Wendy's and so on and on and on...Not that Tommy has noticed "Arnold Layne is my favourite song of all time you know" Yeah Tommy, I know but he still goes on to tell me why. As he is babbling on I notice two girls in a car, no idea of the car, no idea about cars either, lots of ideas about girls. Cars and Girls? then ask fucking Prefab Sprout. Girls are my thing, I love them all, I want them all. You know that supermarket that says "Never knowingly undersold"? I've never knowingly knocked a girl back. So whilst Tommy is talking, talking, talking, I'm looking, thinking, salivating. Unfortunately though they are in a car, so are we and unless you're going to Rutger Hauer them, you're not getting far, unlike Tommy who is bombing down this road faster than my wank fantasies are developing about those girls. And that is saying something.

As we keep on driving another car comes up and its look the one from Ferris Buellers Day Off, a classic film with classic Ferrari. I look over and at first it looks like Catherine or Audrey Hepburn, I can't recall which. She has head scarf on and Jackie Kennedy sunglasses, hood down with cream coloured gloves on the wheel. I'm staring like David Blaine and she is waving at us and tooting her horn. Tommy, mid Pink Floyd lecture, looks in his mirror a couple of times and says "Who the fuck is this? Megan Fox?" Only he could sound angry about that. I tell him to pull over and it first he looks at me as if I'm insane, again, then does. "If this turns out to *be a car-jacking, I'm telling you now, I ain't gonna be happy"*

She pulls up behind us and I can tell right away, she's a happy sort. She bangs on our window and I unwind it slowly, can I help you? "Hello, Irish?" What? "I saw your bumper sticker?" Ah, Tommy's wife is from Cavan. "I'm Mary, born Glasgow, lived in Donegal, now here!" She put her hand out to shake it and I could feel Tommy's eyes burning into the back of my head. "You're Scottish then?" Aye. "Unbelievable, I've never met any over here" and then the regular senses kick in, this girl has hit the jackpot if she's looking for some home comforts. "What can we do for you Sweetie?" Tommy, blunt as ever, "Well my oil thingmie isn't working and I hadn't passed a garage, sorry, gas station in ages, "I'll fix it", Tommy was out and at em. So of course, I ask what her story is and it comes "I invented the App that delivers Newspapers to your smart phone, made a fortune and I'm out here spending it" Really....I felt myself go all a quiver when came closer, nice and cool my son, nice and cool, she got to my ear and said "And I've met a million guys like you and didnae come 3000 miles to shag one of them, so nae offence, your pal is nice though" I liked her style but there were two fatal flaws in her defence, 1) Tommy loves his wife and his wife alone and 2) I'd heard the same spiel before and it's always more of a challenge than warning. Ok then, cool, thing is Tommy is taken and I'm slicker than Slick Rick, so don't deny yourself right away, ok? She laughed, she'd heard this patter before but it's a marathon my friends, not a sprint.

"It's fixed" Tommy was back and raring to go. "Thanks, here's my card, I'm heading to Miami, give me a call" and with that she was gone. I looked at the card and it said

"Mary Coyle inc", I looked back at her go and thought it was only half time.

I'd always been more of a Led Zeppelin guy. Can you honestly tell me that Immigrant Song doesn't get you up every time you hear it? The more I read and hear about Led Zeppelin the more I am convinced that Jimmy Page, Robert Plant, John Paul Jones&John Bonham are or were not human. I'm not a guy for dissecting lyrics like Manson did with The Beatles, and if I was, I fucking hate California anyway, so I'm not sending anyone there so slay Lindsay Lohan or whoever, I love her with all my heart, but Led Zep wrote the best fucking songs of all time. Read the lyrics of Whole Lotta Love and tell me I'm wrong. You wanna get yourself pumped for a date with a new girl, then it has to be Houses of The Holy, and if you wanna separation fuck, That's The Way. Most would got for Go Your Own Way by Fleetwood Mac, but I'm not most fucking people, and as Ricky Roma says "I believe in contrary public opinion". Besides, this is a lesson you're getting my friend, don't question your Uncle. Also, this is not the end of the lesson because like Shangri la beneath the summer moon, I will return again.

"You see at the time in Pink Floyd they were doing Pop songs" Tommy was back to pontificating. "The song tells a story of a guy who was in Cambridge was stealing woman's clothes at night from their back yard washing lines. The best line is "two to know, two to know" I guess Syd Barrett was in tune with that as there was probably more men out there wearing woman's clothing... This must have put people in fear of some sicko. I just think it's funny and the sound is great like from where Pink Floyd started and it's before they

found their psychedelic sound"

The man was on a roll. He can talk Tommy although he can go for ages and you think "What the fuck is he talking about?" He can ramble on for hours and his story still has him at the breakfast table. Then one day he will just say something like "So I was talking to my sister today" and you're like "What sister?". Who is he? Somebody. Why is here? He owns the place. Where is he from? Centuries of tradition.

7- "It's better to live one day as a Lion than 100 years as a Lamb"

"We need gas" and with that he had veered the car into a gas station like an Indy 500 pit stop. As I got to stretch the legs a guy "hey, what the fuck you doing?" I looked over and then looked behind me, he was looking just beyond me, then at me. What's the problem? "No cell phones here, it messes with the machinery" Machinery? You got two gas pumps and a fucking coke machine? "Yeah, one time this guy got his coins jammed in it, it was his cell phone, that's why I don't have one" He was harmless. I clocked the name tag on his boiler suit "J Daniel", so I asked him to throw a couple of bottles of the family product in the back and he looked at me like I meant gas. "By the way, if you're look for a good place to visit, New Orleans, fantastic". Thanks man. He reminded me of Steve Martin I think but I wasn't sure. Tommy, always in a hurry when he was in a hurry, breezed out, and said "Leave Leatherface for the locals", he had heard nothing of what had been seen but he was happy to chastise the man all the same. As we left, J Daniel gave us a thumbs up and I thought "Nice guy, just mis-understood"

"One Slip is a great song I think it's about when David Gilmour saw his wife Polly Samson for the first time. It's got the best words for seeing a beautiful woman from across a room. It starts with "A restless eye across a weary room". and that's it from there with many things" Why didn't he say he wanted to fuck her?. Tommy looked at me to see if I was serious and when he saw I was said "You and me are gonna talk soon"

Thanks Tommy. We never normally do t

"Don't judge David Jon Gilmour BY YOUR FUCKING MORALS!!!!!!!!!!!!"

Take it easy.

"I'm calmer than you are"

He had me with the Walter Sobchak line.

He did allow the occasional other sing and right then we were rocking to Cuntry Disco by Happy Mondays and sung, of course, by the great Shaun William Ryder.

I should explain what he said about the hiding under the dashboard at this point. See his last car was a Toyota I know that, I also know it was never the fucking car in front. Anyway, it made this weird buzzing noise, that sounded like a bomb was approaching you or like the car in the movie Uncle Buck? So, when we used to drive home from the city at night, as we got onto Skyline Drive, it's like the fucking Blair Witch Project there at the best of times, the noise would be incredible from the car so when we approached the houses, you'd see people at their windows going nuts, wondering if the Russians were coming. Fine at night, Jersey has the darkest sky on this planet, but during the day people would hear the car coming, stop for a second and think "That's it, that's the fucking car that wakes me up every night, that's the car that has driven me to a nervous breakdown" and they'd rush out to see who was driving it. So we hid under the dashboard. And as for driving them to a nervous breakdown? It barely got us to the city.

We're not in the car now though, we're in one of those tank type cars where you feel 15 feet from the pavement and we're listening to yet another of Tommy's theories on Pink Floyd.

"Dark Side of the Moon is great as it runs along with The Wizard of Oz. When the MGM lion roars for third time you press play on your CD. Things like the Great Gig in the Sky go along with the tornado, certain things that are said in songs happen in the movie like Dorothy falling off a fence. The whole thing was thought to be Roger Waters' master plan but he never admitted it. I think it was all Allan Parsons doing.

The bells go off in Time when that woman who plays the witch shows up to take Toto, She also shows up as the witch when in the song Us and Them they say the words "Black and Blue". The good witch Glinda and the wicked witch of the west banter back and forth when they say "which is which and who is who".

"There are other things that go on like sound effects"

I should explain more, I don't not like Pink Floyd, I love a lot of their stuff and "Wish You Were Here" is in my top 5 but Floyd is tainted a bit for me though, I suppose it's something to do with the fact my dad played Dark Side of the Moon about 300 times. It's not music for kids and the song with the clocks on it in particular used to really get on my breasts. Everything after that has got worse, particularly The Wall which is up there for my least favourite album of all time. I tried to listen to them since and got into some of it and I quite like some of the really early stuff, but there's definitely a flavour about some of the 70's albums which suggests self-indulgent shite. I do, on the other hand, think certain music has to grow on you, the amount of stuff I like now that I had no clue even existed 10 years ago (CCR, Alan Parsons Project etc), it's not quite the Stevie Wonder syndrome with Pink Floyd where everything was brilliant then suddenly for no apparent reason, awful, but my theory is that the stuff from the late 70s early 80s won't be likeable for us until about 2015.

I won't share this with Tommy though as I'll never hear the end of it from here to West Virginia and I already have "Country Road-Take me home" going over and over in my head. That ever happen to you? You hear a name, it's from a song and you can't get rid of that song? It's worse for me, anytime I hear a different accent, I end up trying to replicate it. I dated an Irish girl and spent most of the time sounding like Colin Farrell. Pissed.

8-"Always be nice to bankers. Always be nice to pension fund managers. Always be nice to the media. In that order."

"By the way, I'm Shelley's Bar last week, $.4.50, I run into Steve Delgado who I haven't seen since his wedding eight years ago. He married a girl who lived in Jackson Heights and was better than everyone else well, that's what she thought, and Steve has been a prisoner. So he sneaked out for a beer that turned to four in the old neighborhood. It was only out of luck that I ran into him so a few more drinks went down, when John Gardener walks in. Now I haven't seen this guy for about as long as I have seen Steve. He orders a beer and says hello to a few guys at the other end of the bar and started making his way down to my end. I turn to tell Steve look who's here and he has gone to the bathroom. I start talking to John how's his mom, brother, sister the usual shit that you don't really care about. Steve, John and I all worked together at the local bar as busboys. I noticed Steve was back and said "hey look who's here" Steve had a strange look on his face and said "hey" So I turned back to John to talk and I see a strange look on his face. A fist passes mine and hits John in his face. The next minute Steve is hitting John yelling "you fucked my girlfriend, you fucked my girlfriend" I grab Steve in this one sided fight and take him to the floor. At this point I am thinking what is he talking about? It seems that 10 years ago John slept with Steve's girlfriend Danielle and was now getting him back.

After everything has quieted down and Steve was sent home and John giving some ice for his face. After all this excitement I had a thought, wow I fucked his girlfriend too when they were dating"

I wanna stop for Crab Cakes. Well that is, I wanna stop at a Crab Cake place. We're in Maryland, you gotta, right? Linthicum Heights, home of G&M, is the only place to go for them. I order Fried Clam strips, Scallops and Calamari. Fuck you I missed breakfast. Tommy orders Cream of Crab Soup and a deluxe Hamburger. His one point of protest at granting my wish of stopping at a seafood restaurant for lunch. I've been here before and I like it but the best seafood I ever tasted was in Montauk, at the Crow's Nest, even with the $7 beer. They would say it was "East Hamptons", I say Montauk. They can say what they want though; the fucking food should be served in Heaven. Come to think of it, Montauk is Heaven, but that's another story...

I am reminded of a guy I know, Mick Donnelly, when I see this guy come in with a ridiculous suicide blonde hair style, Mick it works for Clooney...

We finish up, I pay, Tommy hits the bathroom, he sure does piss a lot for a skinny guy and we're on the road again. Not far though, we have to make a stop in Maryland that, for once, Tommy isn't complaining about, "This is gonna be fun". I had arranged to me two of my old teachers, Pat and George, Pat lived there, George was visiting him, we were passing through, so it seemed stupid not to catch up. "I'll be able to find out all your college shit hahahahahahaha" Sometimes Tommy was off his fucking head. Only last week he went to see his niece run track, showed up late and so drove his car round the side of track shouting encouragement at her as he drove. Yeah that is as bad as it sounds. We had arranged to meet in a diner until I told Tommy, and he didn't hesitate "I'm not stopping at Mel's

Diner, tell them to make it a bar that has a jukebox and imported beer" Ok, so that was done and we drove up to the place and Tommy sat for five minutes "looking it over" before we went in. I'd seen George over the years but hadn't seen Pat in 12 years. He looked the same, wee bit greyer, but still a Handsome Dan, and George was still exactly the same, fidgety but happy. Being Shitkicker, USA, it was $3 a beer, line em up. I remember the first time I met Pat, I was 23, no prospects, and had just woken up to the fact that I needed some. So I went back to school and first class, first day, Pat was the teacher. All the other students, bar one guy in his 50s, were 18 and the age gap at that time was huge, they still called the teacher Sir and asked to go to the toilet, I'd been drinking in bars for nine years. The first thing Pat did was write his name on the board. In orange chalk. After he did, he turned and said "Does anyone object to the orange chalk by the way?" I put my hand up, smiled and said "Aye me" and he looked right at me and said "Good" and smiled back. As starts go to college careers, they don't get much better. One other thing about Pat, the week after Celtic stopped 10 in a row, I went on a four day bender, only pitching up at college on the Wednesday. As Pat took the register he said my name, I replied, and he looked up "Celebrating?" I nodded "Good" and he smiled.

George I'd known for years before college, through political beliefs and marching, again, like Hosey. When I turned up at college and he saw me it may have passed his mind that he'd pissed someone off and a word was needed, that was more believable than me going to college that's for sure. What I love about George though he is wee non aggressive guy but stands up for what he believes in, he will take to the streets to prove that and in the kind of environment we were in and opposition we faced, you'll always be ok in my book. Which is this your reading now. My God I'm clever.

We had some drinks and Pat said there was a Scottish Games tomorrow, did we want to stay for it? George nodded enthusiastically. Although I am Scottish and love a lot about Scotland, I'll never be your Tartan Army "Whae's like us?" Scot. With a big Irish heritage, I've always nodded more towards that, and so you'd find me much happier on the streets of Belfast than Inverness. Of course, George, being George, couldn't let that go, "We must embrace our Scottish culture, our enemies would like nothing more than for us to shun it but we are all Jock Tamson's Bairns" Pat laughed in that "Here we go" way and Tommy was loving it although keeping quiet. I had to wade in, "George, I love you but fur fucks sake, our whole lives we have been treated like shite in Scotland, we had to march for years and years just to get one of best Scottish men who ever lived some recognition, our fitba team gets derided by bigots all over the country, they attack what they perceive as our schools, the media nitpicks at us, demonizes us, undermines us and fucking hates us, most of the country cannie fucking stand us or our very existence and you want me ME! to go to some Highland Games pish and hang about with all these fucks who are gonnie tell me aw misty-eyed what a great place Scotland is? I've been fighting my whole life against them and for some years to get as far away from them as possible. Until they apologise for years of bigotry and racism against our people, until they say sorry for allowing a football club to operate a policy of apartheid for decades, until they give us equality on every level, they can Pogue Mahone"

There was a silence until Pat chimed in "That a No for a games then?" I nodded. "Good" and he smiled.

9- "Don't carry a gun. It's nice to have them close by, but don't carry them. You might get arrested."

"Did you hear about Ricci?" This could be anything. "Stupid Motherfucker is in court last week, some shit with his wife and he calls me up and says the Judge is Scottish, can you do anything, so I've got you on speed dial when it hits me, what the fuck is he talking about? he says the guys name is Paul Scott, so he's Scottish. I almost jumped in the car, went down there and strangled him" What the fuck was it all about anyway? "His wife got a restraining order on him. It's his fucking fridge that needs to do that, do them both a favour the fat bastard" Tommy has a story about everyone at some point or another and almost all of them end with him wanting to or very nearly killing the person involved. Hey, you don't become Tommy by writing letters to the paper about your problems.

We're stopping in Charlotte tonight. She's not a hooker by the way, it's a place in North Carolina although it makes me think wouldn't be great to have someone in North Carolina called Charlotte? Where you could stop, fuck her for the night, then head down to fucking Florida? I do have a girl there by the way, her name is Melanie, and she's a nice girl, sweet, huge ass. To look at her from the waist up, hell you might even fall in love, but waist down she looks like she's trailing two beach balls as ass cheeks. Roll back a bit though, let's not be picky here, I'll have two on hands on and one dick between those ass cheeks pretty soon.

Tommy though, still only has eyes for another type of pink...

"Did you know, in The Wall Bob Geldof is sitting on the floor in the bathroom of the concert hall before he goes on as Pink and is reciting lyrics for their next album The Final Cut"

I can tell he's getting tired though, he's driving like a lunatic so he can get his head down and not like I want to. The inevitable happens and we get flashed by a cop car and we pull over "Anything outstanding?" Tommy asks, No, "Good". One cop gets out, there are two of them, and there's something weird about this cop, he looks human. "Licence and registration", Tommy hands it over and says "Yeah sorry about that, my man here has a hot date in Charlotte, you probably know her, Melanie?" The cop looks at him as if he's crazy and says "from the fourth ward?" Tommy lights up "Yeah!" oh for fucks sake "Yeah I know her" and he hands back the documents and I see the badge, P O'Neil, and he waves over his partner, who walks over and he tells him "Hey Steven, they know Melanie" he lights up "from the fourth ward?" "YEAH!" they all exclaim. He has a badge that says "S O'Neil" and so, to get back at them, I say "what are you, brothers?" and amazingly, the cunts are. "Yeah I got my little brother in a couple of years ago" Steven says. Fucking inbred cunts. We talk more and they seem ok, in fact, better. "Listen, you guys partying tonight?, We can get you anything you want, blow, crank, chronic, hookers, oh, wait, you got Melanie, right?" He laughs, yeah keep laughing. "Na, we're good guys" Tommy says to his new best buddies, "Unless you got a a few bottles of GreyGoose in there?" and laughs himself, "Sure, Paul, get them out the trunk", Paul looks up "The big ones or the quarts? I'll get the Marlboros as well, I know Melanie likes em". The fucking Carolinas huh?

We hit Charlotte, Melanie is standing at her door waving, Tommy looks at her and says to me "What the hell is wrong with you?" and then we get out, say out Hellos and Tommy hits the sack. Charlotte is one boring fucking place and I am grateful for Melanie. She was a real homely girl and yeah she wasn't the best looking but fuck Tommy, she had class and was kind and was putting us up in the middle of the night. maybe I should just go through now and smother him with a pillow, yeah and never be seen on this planet again, I'll pass. Melanie had scones, tea and a worried look. She asked if I was ok and I was like "With Colonel behind me? How can I not be?" She smiled but didn't seem convinced. Oh fuck off, it's been a long drive Mel, can't I just say "open sesame" and you will? Pretty please? She took the cups away and put some Led Zeppelin on, a welcome relief. Dancing Days was the track which made me wonder why she'd gone straight to track five of Houses Of The Holy but when she started to lap dance, I couldn't have cared less why. She moved slowly towards me, a hint of being alone too much in her face but she'd also clearly had a drink which was Ok by me, some men (Yeah you Paul) get put off by shit like that, me? I fucking love it. When I looked at here properly she was a thing a beauty, Ok I had drink too, and I loved her really and as I pulled her top over her head, me now towering over over, her tits bobbled like the lotto balls. She slowly pulled me to the bedroom as Robert Plant reggaed up for The Ocean and before long I was in her arms like a baby in the womb. Melanie, I love you baby, you're as good a friend a man could ever have and it's your loyalty that makes you, never lose that sweetheart. She told me after we fucked that she was getting married next year. I just hope the guy has thighs as strong as me.

We slept all night and awoke to an almighty banging, no not us, Tommy. "Any fucking Coffee around here, I got a long drive" We looked at each other and I gave her a log kiss, lingering, whilst she jerked me off.

One Melanie satisfied later, we're on our way to the Sunshine State. I was beginning to unwind. I normally can't relax but Melanie had calmed, I hope her marriage is great and if not I'll kill her husband. Well I'll get Tommy to. "What was she like then?" Who? "Fucking Rosie O'Donnell from Charlotte". Good. "Yeah, right". How do you answer that? I once got a train down to fucking Florida and although everyone thought I was crazy, I loved it. It left Penn Station at 3pm on the Tuesday and got into Orlando on the Wed at 11am. Fuck me I've done longer on the 32 bus. So I'm on this train and I've got a dinner reservation for 7pm, see sounding better already right? So, cologned up, I make my way to the restaurant car, and my table is ready and then I see distress on the waitress face. Anyone from the underclass like myself is well used to this, you're waiting on the inevitable "Where the fuck do you think you're going" pull. This time, no, "Excuse me Sir, I am so sorry to bother you, please excuse the inconvenience, we have a young lady also traveling alone and we wondered if you would mind sharing a table with her?" Now, this would be the part in the movie where the guy would be pissed, then he would look over and see she was gorgeous and then rapidly change his mood, right? Right. Except this ain't a movie, I agreed before I even had the chance to look her over, that's how I roll, you must know that by now? What the fuck have you been reading? I'll say now I didn't fuck her or even get a tug under the table, what I did get though was a number, a Florida number, and I've just

laid it on Tommy that I am going to call it now from the car.
After a long pause he says "You're serious? we are down here
on business for Christ sake, what did you say she did, is this
the air hostess? fucking air-head more like, we don't need
that shit, not on this trip, too distracting, no, it's no-go, no-
go, that Mary was crazy" She's a lawyer. "Oh. Yeah, give her
a call, who knows when you need a lawyer right?" His
immediate change of tone unnerved me but I rang the
number anyway, "Hello, Adrianna De Moss speaking" I
explained who I was but to her I was "The nice guy from the
train", it was kinda patronising but not a total get to fuck. I
told her I'd be in fucking Florida tomorrow morning and
asked if she fancied Brunch which gave Tommy an
expression like I'd just asked for a three way with him and
his brother. She said she would check with work and call me
back. A brush off? Yeah, maybe. We'd talked all sorts of shit
on the train but I knew right away this woman was not a
skittle to my bowling ball and she did make me think. I
hoped she would call. "What the fuck would a lawyer be
doing getting a train to fucking Florida? I don't like it" She
told me she hated flying. "Oh fuck that, there's no turbulence
in first class my friend" He had a point, I flew back from the
Orlando trip first class and the service was as good as Rick's
on 33rd, that's all I am saying. By the time I got off the plane
at JFK, my luggage wasn't the only thing getting carried off
the plane.

We hit speed down the highway and I saw a sign that said
"Jacksonville 26 miles" so I knew then we were in fucking
Florida. we had made good time for once so Tommy actually
suggested we stop for breakfast. Our incredibly early start
and Tommy's driving saw us get here in four hours and it

wasn't even 8am. We pull into this diner in a place called Yulee, actually it was a bit to the left of it, near a place called Amelia Island. A 50's style diner, it reminded of the one in Pulp Fiction where Travolta and Thurman win the dance competition. Tommy said he needed to make a few calls and made his way to row of phone booths on the right of it. I went in to get us a table when I heard a voice behind "Give me your wallet and watch", I thought it was Tommy fucking around but I turned to see this red neck fuck standing there with a knife like the one Crocodile Dundee had. I told him to fuck off but was then grabbed from behind by another guy and realised this was a fucking ambush, "Shut the fuck up Yankee boy or I'll snap your spine like a twig". This was the second time in my life I had been mugged, I was in Amsterdam in 1992 with a couple of guys, one being Chris O'Neill, we were walking through the red light district at night with three adults and turned a corner only to see Chris, at the front of the group, get jumped by three guys with knives. I ran towards him, safe in the knowledge that I had three big burly adults behind me except they had ran away. A vital life lesson as my money, passport (one year thankfully) and match ticket for Borussia Dortmund v Celtic were stolen from me at knife-point. Being 18 and thinking I knew all, I know now I could have died that night and I also know now that I could die right now. Thing is, what I didn't have in Amsterdam, what the red necks didn't realise I had here, was Tommy. Suddenly a voice, "If you pricks ever want to see another Lynyrd Skynyrd concert, release your hands and get on your knees" Tommy stood mightily in front of these cunts, by now both of them shaking and trying to calm him and make him not shoot the gun he was holding. "You motherfuckers just made the biggest mistake of your lives"

Tommy tied them up and proceeded to beat both of them with the butt of his gun for a good five minutes. They were barely alive when we left them but still mumbling insults. I was shocked by the raw violence. Seeing violence up close is not nice, even a boxing match, is sanitised on TV by commentators, so when I walked back to the car, I was shaken by it all, numb. I sat in the car and was snapped out of it by something familiar, it was a song

Big wheels keep on turning
Carry me home to see my kin
Singing songs about the Southland
I miss Alabamy once again
And I think it's a sin, yes

Tommy was singing and smiling "God damn, this has been a great trip"

10- "All I wanted was to be was what I became to be"

A Facebook message had came in on my phone from Gary Haley wanting to know about a new project and I replied as we hit 90 mph. Gary was always an "Ok" text guy but his expression in voice and on paper was incredible. Genius/Nutjob I guess.

The talk of business by Tommy though made me think, what the fuck was he talking about? I thought we were down here for the ride and to pick up something for the never ending work on his fucking house? What the fuck was he playing at now?

"I have an idea that I am going to try and develop down here"

Oh no. "Go on?"

"You know how New York water is the best right?"

Rrrriiiiight?

"And they say that's why you can't get good pizza or bread down south or out west?"

Mmmmm.

"Well, I had this idea. If I can get like 10 trucks to begin with, milk trucks you know? The ones that carry like a million litres of milk?"

Yeeeah.

"Right, I get these trucks and instead of filling them with milk, I fill them with New York water, ship them down to fucking Florida all day every day, back and forth, right, start my own bakery down there, that does pizza also, people hear about it, you make a website, email and shit and before long we'll have trucks and bakeries all over America, all with the good water, none of that California or fucking Florida shit"

At this point I felt it wasn't time to point out the million fucking reasons why it wouldn't work.

I thought we were meeting Aisling down there and there's no way she would....fuck me she's standing there smiling, she knows all about it. My phone goes, it's Chas, telling me all was good in The Bronx.

I was about to tell Tommy this when my phone rang again, I half cursed it until I saw the name flash up "Flash Lawyer", it was Adrianna, "Hey, so I'm free, you still want to grab Brunch?" I feel this was God rewarding me for 22 hours in a car with Tommy.

He'd clearly been thinking about his plan a lot and it was abundantly crystal to me why he had agreed so readily to go do to fucking Florida for a week the cunt, but I didn't want to rain on his parade, I'd done enough of that with Melanie, so I asked him, what you going to call this business then?
He looks at me, he thinks I am all for this, he actually thinks I am buying all this and he pauses, he's reveling in this moment no doubt about that the cocky bastard, before he

finally speaks

"Ah, that's the easy part, Roger's Water, get it!"

And I finally did.

Part of a book of short stories. The cunt normally writes about Celtic, now he's writing aboot fucking road trips tae Florida? Tosser. That said, he was always a fucking waster so at least the cunt is daeing something. I'll always see him as a waster but.

I think aboot this for a bit until she appears in my line of sight.

I think back to last night, I'd gone to *Rasta Baby* and clocked this other white guy toking away. I nodded at him, through the haze of smoke and dreadlocks and made my way to buy some quality cannabis. After my purchase he beckoned me over so I went. "Strangers huh?" was his first line as he nodded at all the Rastafarians around us. I nodded and he laughed. As I started to skin up I could tell he felt the need to hit me with a story. He was American and affable, not a normal combination. Gave me the sense that he knew the score but also liked to keep his own counsel, before revealing it like an atomic bomb:

Place is Woodside, Queens in the mid 70's a heavily tough working class hood.. Once a huge Irish born and Irish American area is now becoming home to a new group. Hispanics..South Americans mainly Colombian and a large

*group of Dominicans & Puerto Ricans Americans trying to
escape the slums of Northern Manhattan & da southern
Bronx . Now I'm not gonna tell you I have nothing against
these people, I do. But I also understand where these people
are coming from. See I was the child of immigrants too, we
had to make our way , just like these new people have to. And
yeah its a great country and with a lot of opportunity,
especially if you want to make a fast buck. Legal or illegal .
You see me and my group of pals, we're a rough and tumble
bunch. You had me, Donny & his brother Declan , Jimmy
Buckets[got the name cause he walked around like he was
carrying 2 large buckets] Pat the hat and Jimmy the
murderer [well you can guess how he got that name]. Plus
we had a bunch of guys who hung around with us, who
would do anything for a quick buck. We started out selling
"trey bags" of weed in the local schoolyards after school and
on the weekends. From there we moved on to selling oz's of
weed. Then on to hash, then mescaline & mushrooms. We
had Woodside . Sunnyside and Maspeth on lockdown. No one
sold anything without us getting a cut.*

I recognised the preamble, he was building up his role in
sorting cunts out but I liked it. You don't meet guys like this
now, guys like "Stearns" which he told me to call him.

*Well in comes the "new people", and they bring cocaine with
them. Within a month, these people are making a small
fortune selling coke and weed out of the Mets
houses{Housing scheme }Like I said, I got no problem with
people making money, but ya got to pay taxes. And we own
this area. So I go down to the Mets with Donny, Pat, and 2
other kids to collect on these taxes. We walk through the*

archway, my Aunt Mary used to live on the second floor of the first building. So I know the place like the back of my hand. And I see the first PR standing there, I hey pal you got anything for sale. He said sure what do you need ? I said well 200 bucks will do for a start. He looked at me for a second, then pulled a knife. Pat, to the left of me, just laughed. And said hey spic put that away before you regret it. The guy made a move towards Pat, Pat took out his 38 and shot the guy twice in the leg. Donny ran over and kicked him in the face and then started turning his pockets out. The guy had 20 small packages of coke, 50 nickel bags of weed and about 140 bucks in cash. We collected all and told the guy we would be back for the rest by the end of the week. Told him that we owned the area, and they were more then welcome to sell drugs. Just that we would need our cut.

At this point I felt like I was in The Wanderers, which was great and a huge release from the normal shite I had to listen to.

Saturday arrives, we load up 2 cars of the hardest cunts in all of Woodside. This time we come through the back entrance, we hear a whistle. We know that's a warning that we're coming. All of us are packed, I have my 45 in my waistband. Straight razor in my back pocket. We turn the corner and see 15 hispanic guys standing there. Right away I reach for my gun and so does my whole crew, right off the bat. 10 of the hispanic guys take off. Leaving 5 of them, 2 I can see have small calibre hand guns, walk towards the first guy with a gun and shoot him right above his belly button. Kick his gun away and now put the 45 to the head of the leader of this group and told him that they owed back taxes

*on the dope they were selling. He said we would get nothing
from him and cursed at us in Spanish. Jimmy the murderer
had enough and put 3 bullets in this guys head. Told the
others to empty their pockets and collected 100's in money.
1000's in drugs. Told them we would be back every week to
collect. Next week we show up, the same whistle is blown. We
turn the corner and a brown paper bag is on the ground,
look in the bag. 1000 dollars in 20's. We find out that these
guys have given us a name. White Terror. I think it fits*

The name made me uncomfortable but that washed away
with the mention of "Terror" which took me back to The
Wanderers again. Finishing my joint I could feel Stearns
looking at me for my reaction which was to shake his hand.
I've been in America enough times to know this wasn't a
race thing, it was a fucking money thing, a neighborhood
thing and a take no shit thing. As communities tore
themselves apart in Edinburgh in the 80s and 90s with
Heroin and Thatcher told every cunt that there was nae
such thing as society, I felt strangely pleased to meet this
cunt Stearns. I dabbed my joint out and shook his hand and
he smiled as I left. A smile that says "you know the rules".

I look again and she's standing at my table. It's a beautiful
day and although she blocks out the sun whilst standing
there, I don't care. The place I'm at, Cafe Heuvel on
Prinsengracht, I stumbled upon one day whilst heading for
Vondel Park. It was a time where I had all this weed on me
and didn't know the Coffee Shop etiquette. So I'd decided to
head to Vondel and smoke the lot, only I'd pre rolled them
all and started smoking the first one the way down there
and was both starving and thirsty almost immediately and

spotted this wee place. Nothing better than a cool, golden Heineken to take that sandpaper like taste away from your tongue that Jack Herer weed always gives. Thinking of Jack Herer makes smile and remember Harry's advice when I first came here, I hadn't been since the 90s and asked him for some Coffee Shop advice, instead it unlocked a Harry guide to Amsterdam.

From harrymilne07@gmail.com
To: siddemps@gmail.com

Firstly, do you ken the difference between a Sativa & Indica weed? Most stuff you'll get are a hybrid of both types, but there's a different buzz to the two of them. Anything which is heavier on the indica will be your melting gouching type gear, anything which is more sativa will be your giggly type stone. Worth keeping different things in different pockets I've found because going for the wrong one can be a complete pain in the arse. Most indicas have a more skunky ammonia smell. Honestly, dinnae be shy in asking dealers for advice about what to smoke, very few of them will advise you wrongly, and they usually aren't pushing you to take the dearest stuff but more what you are wanting. Also, get a grinder if you're smoking green, the buds are usually so tightly packed it's going to take fucking ages to get a joint the gither if you huvnae got one. Dinnae spend fortunes on one cause you're liable to lose it, just get something for a couple of euros.

Anyway, Coffee-shops.

Walk out of Centraal and disobey all your instincts and turn right in the opposite direction from the Red Light District :) Walk along for a couple of minutes and you come to Rasta Baby on the main road just opposite the huge bike parking thing. Nice wee chilled place with loads of Rastas smoking big feck off joints in it. Funny enough, loads of reggae are the sounds. Kindae dark in the back, and a nice wee conservatory bit at the front. Wouldnae swear to it, but have a feeling they might sell in bags with different amounts as opposed to per gram. Pretty cheap if I mind right, but the dope is pretty variable in quality. If you're buying just get a gram of something mild.

Just over the canal (Singel) from Rasta Baby are The Doors and The Rokerij (there's more than one Rokerij so I'll call this 1). The Doors is a pretty standard type place with a The Doors theme to it. Cannae mind if I've ever even bought any stuff out of it, so no sure about dope quality etc. Sounds are all Doors all the time when I've been in it, so avoid it if you dinnae like The Doors! No been in much though so could be coincidence.

Next door to it is Rokerij 1. Place is genuinely very cool. All sort of arty Afro design stuff on the walls and ornaments and shit. Definitely visit here. Quality and price of dope in all Rokerijs is the same. I always buy Jack Herer weed from one of them as my standard weed to have with me. Giggly stuff but you can still function which is a decent staple. Wee bit on the dear side, but always decent quality gear. Oh aye, I'm convinced the seats in here are specifically designed to stop you hanging about too long cause they're uncomfy as fuck! They're all really low down so you kindae feel like you're *sitting in a fecking play school.*

Right next to the Rokerij is Harlemerstraat which is the home of Barneys. All of them. Walk along for maybe 5 minutes and you'll see it on the corner facing you on the right hand side. They were a bit up in the air the last time I was there as they had a new place over the road, but I'll try and guide you but all this stuff might have changed. First thing is that there's only one of the three places which actually sells dope. This is so that the other two can sell peeve (as you can't sell both in the same place). No many places about at all where you can smoke and bevvy at the same time, but they're all bars rather than coffee-shops. Anyway, the one on the corner is a sort of cafe with tables outside (you can still smoke). Next door to it is the coffee shop bit, and it is usually rammed. The reason why Barneys is always busy as is because it does a big feck off fry up. Highly recommend the breakfast, but it is properly dear (think it was about €15 the last time I was there). Barneys used to be a greasy spoon type place but it's went kindae upmarket now. Now I've only been in the Barneys opposite the coffee-shop once but think it will be properly busy later on at night. Kindae like a big modern boozer you can have a blow in. Think it was one of the few smoking places I went to which had a tele showing sport but wouldn't swear to that. The dope in Barneys is wildly expensive from memory, and not particularly brilliant imo. Buy stuff elsewhere would be my advice. Nice place though and they don't just do fry ups they've got a decent menu and it's a good place for a Scottish type scran.

The above is my usual first thing in Amsterdam if I'm on an early flight. Couple of quiet wee doobies and strong coffee and either across to the Rokerij or along to Barneys for breakfast. I really like Rasta Baby, and you should definitely pop into the Rokerij 1 even if it's only for a juice cause it's very cool.

I remember digesting this one night and before I got to the end, another email came in from the cunt.

Walk or Tram to Leidseplein
I'll split this up into two bits, I'll go for a couple of places up at Leidsplein first, then to a couple of places on the way to or from it.

Leidseplein

Loads of trams go to it. Cannae mind the numbers, but a 2 and 5 definitely do which you can get from Centraal. When you get to it, it's a square with loads of boozers, restaurants, hotels etc around it. Definitely a big Burger King there. You've usually got someone doing something radge in the square (unicyclists, cunts daeing keepy uppies for a 12 hour shift etc).

This is where The Bulldog is. There's like a nightclub type place on the ground and first floors. No really my thing tbh, and only been in once. The Coffee Shop is a pleasant surprise compared to it afaic. Could be wrong, but think it was one of if not the first coffee-shop in Amsterdam. Dope I had from there was excellent, and reasonably cheap as well. Definitely a place to go to if you're in the vicinity and want to pick something up. Really old fashioned galley type bar (it actually reminds me a bit of Jinglins thinking about it!) and very chilled people in it (might be cause it's hidden away a bit and not that obvious, feck knows).

There's also a Sports Cafe place here next door to The Bulldog (probably, pretty sure it is). They do burgers etc. Loads of teles showing basically everything. This is a place where you can smoke and bevvy, but only upstairs. Usually rammed wi cunts who just wish they were still in Surrey and able to smoke blow but with no other changes. Tables are rammed together and it's no all that pleasant imo. Also, last time I was in Amsterdam Ajax were away to Feyenoord so I went here to watch the game. Thought it would be good crack to catch an Ajax game in an Amsterdam boozer in the square where they celebrate their titles. Honestly, the cunts drinking in the bar looked at me as if I had two heids at wanting to watch Dutch fitba when there was the build-up to some cunt like West Brom against Blackburn on Sky (aye, build-up, there wasn't even a fucking English game on at the time!). I'm no recommending this place in case you hudnae guessed :) What it is useful for though is as a landmark and somewhere to get your bearings from for the next couple of places I will be recommending.

The corner that The Sports Cafe place is on has a street with millions of restaurants/ clubs etc on it. You want to walk along there for 5 minutes (my timings with all of this are suspect as I'm usually melted whilst in Amsterdam so there's going to only be three different times I'll give; 5 minutes (pretty close) 10 minutes (wee bit of a trek) and fecking miles (I need to sit down somewhere and have a joint between start and finish of this journey)). You want to walk *along here and look on your left hand side for a place called Rookies. Think you have to go over one cross street to get there but genuinely no that far. Rookies is barry. Total bar like atmosphere, excellent cunts smoking in the place, pretty cheap and very good quality dope, and top bar staff. Dinnae ken if they ever got their wish to convert somewhere near into a bar but they miss their peeve in here. Used to have a pool table in it, but when the smoking ban came in they had to build a screen between their serving area and a smoking area. So they did and it left no space for a pool table. Their protest about this is to leave the doors between the smoking area and the serving area open at all times. The hash in particular in here is absolutely magic. Oh aye, I've been on the verge of a whitey in here a couple of times. My usual act in that scenario is to get the fuck out into the fresh air, in there I just stayed and got hot chocolate with marshmallows in it (sugar combats all effects of a whitey). The sounds are all the stuff you'll like (Stones, Bowie, Led Zep etc etc). If you only take one recommendation go here at some point.*

As you leave Rookies turn right and head back towards Leidseplein. The cross street I mentioned earlier, turn right on it (have a feeling there's a greek restaurant on the corner here but no 100% on that). Then you have two options, turn first left for more dope, walk straight on another few yards for one of the best music venues I've been in but you won't have any dope. This is my only non dope recommendation. This is a blues club called Old Orleans, which is absolutely superb. The music has been brilliant every time I've been in. Relatively cheap peeve, and about €5 to get in (think that it was maybe free before 11pm then a charge to get in). It's open till at least 4 in the morning anaw.

If you turned left, walk along that street (Lange Leidsedarstraat I think) and on your right is the Rokerij (call it Rokerij 2). Same dope as the other one. You'd like it in there. Total eastern theme and loads of chill-out music. Kind of a Hindu theme with loads of Ganesh statues etc. It also has the slowest moving ceiling fans in the history of the world which are designed to make you stare at them I'm convinced (honestly, about 3 revolutions per minute!). Clientele is pretty mixed, always stacks of tourists in, but last time I was there was in a December and hardly anyone visiting Amsterdam other than me and Fi, and it was still plenty busy with Dutch folk. Good rule of thumb with coffee-shops is go where the Dutch go. Sounds are all chill-out stuff. Place is pretty dark with loads of the lighting just coming from candles. They sell non-alcoholic beer. Which led to the one of my party during a visit who wasn't smoking to go radge when he discovered this as he'd been paying about €4 a pop for pints of it to try and at least make a night of it! Which cracked everyone else up naturally. Another sound place and well worth popping in. If you're coming from the Leidseplein end rather than The Rookies end the street has a McDonald's on the corner. Also, it's unbelievable how many times I've walked past this place and had to double back to get to it after realising. I've no idea how it happens as it's an open frontage with blue lighting at the front! Anyway, be aware you can miss it, but I've no idea how but it's been at least 5 times that has happened to me!

That'll do Leidseplein. Other stuff about the area, there's still loads of tourists but it's much more likely to be hoaching with locals than the red light. Just over the road (and a canal which loads of boat tours leave from) next to the Marriot is

Vondelpark which you should visit (looks tiny from the entrance but when you go in and walk for a couple of minutes it totally opens up) if the weathers awright. Also, this is about your closest busy area for visiting the Van Gogh and Rijksmuseum (I'll cover them later) which are a good 10 minutes walk away. to get there from here walk past the massive casino and turn right at the Rijksmuseum. Oh aye directly opposite the entrance to Vondelpark is an Irish boozer called The Aran or something like that. Nice view onto the canal and has a terrace etc. Does a scran. Just outside there in the wee square bit is a massive chess board which usually has folk hustling naive cunts who think they are good at chess (and aye, that'll be me).

That'll be me for the night btw! Will cover other bits the morn. Might no actually do the Red Light cause I'm no there enough to be able to make any recommendations!

That's typical of the cunt. He gives you a users guide of how to get and remain high for as long as possible and then tries to make you feel guilty for visiting the Red Light District. That was the thing see, I'd been to Amsterdam before, a few times with the fitba en-route to places and one memorable visit in 2001 when Celtic rolled all over Ajax. The thing is I'd only really been in the RLD on these trips so my other Amsterdam knowledge was poor. Also the Amsterdam and RLD of the late 80s early 90s was a different place. I can mind when the walk from Centraal Station along Nieuwebrugsteeg to the RLD was dangerous as fuck, any time of day. Now tourists flaunt along there with huge cameras and bigger wallets and no one bats an eyelid. Similarly there was always little side streets off Oudezijds, both sides of canal, you could slip away to and have the time for your life for half an hour. Do that now and you'll have six folk from Nebraska watching you haggle whilst some blogger will want you to share your experiences after you've emptied.

She sits down and we order meatballs. They are great here, tangy, spicy or sweet. I order her a Heineken and the waitress smiles. She's beautiful. Mid 50's, look of Honor Blackman about her. That's the waitress like. I'm thinking of the RLD again, the other main difference there now is the women. Most are drop dead gorgeous. That was never the case. Sure you had your few who were good looking but most had that perfumed naughty desperate thing going on, now the whole area looks like a holding pen for Playboy. That's what happens when you get world-wide recession, you need to be at the very top of your game to make money. Even on the fucking game.

Actually, I've just noticed that they serve four types of meatballs here, Tapas style, and all are great, like the Heineken. Beer is great but on a hot day, after a spliff, sitting outside, with a great looking woman opposite you, then Heineken is a marvel. This is my walk on part in the war.

It's in moments like this I feel reflective, think back, wish other cunts could be here. No that cunt Harry though, he'd be sitting here like Prince Hendrik the cunt. When we all know that there's only one Henrik and he is king. Then again I know that's not true, I have another.

In reflecting, I think of my auld man. He died October 6th 2008. My Ma ey said he would die in the boozer but he actually died in Mathesons Bakers. Jist collapsed one day and that was it. His saving grace was he never saw that mob win the league in 2009, 2010 and 2011. Then again he never saw my son, Henrik, born on Sep 26th 2009. That's another Henrik in my life like. Named after his Mum. Well, that's what she tells cunts.

The funny thing is when I met his Mum, I was going through a really bad time and she was adding to it but then this guy, don't know if you mind him, Ferris Moran, telt me how to go efter her and I did. Cunt even sent me the hiries. We went doon to Rothesay and got stranded there and I'd had that last fiver oan me already but a telt her I wanted to stay and watch the sun go down then come back up and she said it sounded good. I never had another bolt oan me bar that fiver but I did huv that letter fae Ferris. Maybe I should huv hud one of those letters that seem all the rage the noo that basically jist says "I'm loaded, honestly, gies mair money but".

Sounds like the new form of bank robbery to me.

I look up at the sky and feel alive.

It's great to be alive.

My Shangri-La beneath the summer moon, I will return again…Just like the Celtic.

And Doyle.

Postscript

Montreal. Friday. 1994. The letter.

Fergus McCann.. "What Is my Motivation for doing This..?"

"First, as a Celtic Supporter I want things changed for the better I believe I can provide the means to help achieve this.

Second, I believe a well-financed, well managed Celtic is a good Investment.

I would expect to make some return.

Third, I believe I can apply my abilities and experience, along with my strong Interest, directly towards managing the Club's affairs - principally its business activities - successfully over a five year period."

Aye Fergus, The Bunnit Dunnit..

No punches pulled, No Deadline Deadlines,

No Tales of conquest or superiority..

Some saw a strange wee man with a master plan.

There it was, the beginnings of what we now know were the start of the recovery.

The complete overhaul of the Celtic Movement which as we know today, has culminated In a fine bill of health amid stranger times.

Aye, The Bunnit,

He grabbed oor braces and hoisted us up though kicking and screaming at times, to firstly survival and as progressed, to positive strength..

There was pain, much pain..

Not all saw the wee guy with anything other than suspicion..

Options.. ?

Not many..

The status quo at the time ?

An unreasonable thought..!

Fergus had something steely, something resolute,

His Vision took time to warm too, but Celtic supporters all too often fobbed off and excused, decided to show that Inbuilt faith.

The Celtic support led by deep root, led by staunch heart, led by men that would not " haud their weesht.." "Sit oan there chorus n verse" or " care aboot soapy bubble"

Had brought the Club to Compass Point- Fergus..

The heroic writers and readers of the fan mags and zines..

clamored to voice the true extent to Inner core of Outer voice..

The baying mob would not be quelled with a nod or wink.!

No funny trooser dance was enough to silence the faithful,

A handshake was a thing of suspicion for those of genuine belief,

No Cash cows to buy off the Bhoyant bulls..

This was a time of acceptance..for denial no longer cut It.

Acceptance that the support were the true foundation and only required the Girder with which to seal with concrete..

Solidifying forever that which is the heritage.

As the last days, hours drew near, the Kingdom shook like never before..

Media parasites lambasted every shade of Green and urged that devastating end, although under guise of concern for some.

If Celtic were to be re-built then all must be as one..

Unity was felt like never before..

Those demonstrations, those hoarse voices and weary speakers, those pen wizards, Informing, Scathing and embracing..

Mustered and Rallied every corner of God's Green lands..

They stirred the passion and demanded the truth, no fear of pain..

Pain was a light relief for what might be such Is the deep set desire for Our Celtic.

Simple truth and Pennance and we felt our Kinship.

The Bhoys and Ghirls Brothers and Sisters needed trust, Honour, Integrity..

They needed the Bunnit.

He offered that with an honesty most were kept from and once accepted moved slowly into all hearts and minds overcoming clashes and hurdles that made many wonder yet again, Yet still they stood firm and did not falter..

The old family dynasty's retreating almost un-noticed past not a second glance..

Their time of damage had been.

Those days, taught us, each and every Celtic man and woman the generations to come.

They taught us to trust ourselves,

Our instincts Our Celtic Pride.

It's a matter of Historical fact now the trials and tribulations, on that forward march to the present Celtic Family...

There is none like it, and those apart from It, Know It Inside themselves!

Those that tore at it with jealous rage,

In any way they could

Those that had not from birth felt this Celtic love, without the understanding of truly what it was.

Those that saw It as enemy..

A love that now as table turns,

Eats like hatred does,

It scorches at that misery being visited to Rivaled Neighbour as a bone gnawing pain this present day.

Across the way, that other semi-detached shackle that enjoys the status of the Loud and Crass relation In the Glasgow Derby, to which they desperately cling Onto...

It Lies breeched In laborious position..

It bleeds from a far more serious wound, most probably mortal..

It's self-inflicted,

Still it harms itself,

A support blinded by many, many, years of unfounded superior belief,

Unable to wrench itself from that abyss, purely due to a strange refusal to accept the DNA of success, is not preserved solely for themselves.

They lash and bite out and bark, failing to see the need for the Bunnit type figure, the strength of Character that rose Celtic from the burning Embers.

They waltz into crisis after crisis relying on hope that being the peepil will be enough...

Lorenzo Wordsmith (@LWordsmith)